Nakshatras

The Ultimate Guide to the 27 Lunar Mansions of Vedic Astrology

© Copyright 2021

The contents of this book may not be reproduced, duplicated or transmitted without direct written permission from the author.

Under no circumstances will any legal responsibility or blame be held against the publisher for any reparation, damages, or monetary loss due to the information herein, either directly or indirectly.

Legal Notice:

This book is copyright protected. This is only for personal use. You cannot amend, distribute, sell, use, quote or paraphrase any part or the content within this book without the consent of the author.

Disclaimer Notice:

Please note the information contained within this document is for educational and entertainment purposes only. Every attempt has been made to provide accurate, up to date and reliable complete information. No warranties of any kind are expressed or implied. Readers acknowledge that the author is not engaging in the rendering of legal, financial, medical or professional advice. The content of this book has been derived from various sources. Please consult a licensed professional before attempting any techniques outlined in this book.

By reading this document, the reader agrees that under no circumstances is the author responsible for any losses, direct or indirect, which are incurred as a result of the use of information contained within this document, including, but not limited to, —errors, omissions, or inaccuracies.

Your Free Gift (only available for a limited time)

Thanks for getting this book! If you want to learn more about various spirituality topics, then join Mari Silva's community and get a free guided meditation MP3 for awakening your third eye. This guided meditation mp3 is designed to open and strengthen ones third eye so you can experience a higher state of consciousness. Simply visit the link below the image to get started.

https://spiritualityspot.com/meditation

Contents

INTRODUCTION 1
PART ONE: THE 27 LUNAR MANSIONS 3
CHAPTER 1: INTRODUCTION TO THE 27 LUNAR MANSIONS 4
    RELATIONSHIP BETWEEN NAKSHATRAS AND ZODIAC SIGNS 6
    THE 27 NAKSHATRAS 7
    CATEGORIZATIONS OF THE 27 NAKSHATRAS 12
CHAPTER 2: A CLOSER LOOK AT NAKSHATRAS 14
    THE THREE GUNAS 14
    NAKSHATRAS AND THE THREE GUNAS 16
    CONNECTION BETWEEN LORDS OF THE NAKSHATRAS AND THE GUNAS 18
    PADAS AND NAVAMSAS 20
    THE 27 NAKSHATRAS AND THEIR DILEANATIONS 21
PART TWO: THE LUNAR MANSIONS TRILOGY 35
CHAPTER 3: JANMA NAKSHATRAS: THE FIRST NINE
NAKSHATRAS 36
    THE FIRST NINE NAKSHATRAS – JANMA NAKSHATRAS 37
CHAPTER 4: ANUJANMA NAKSHATRAS: THE SECOND
NAKSHATRA GROUP 46
    INFLUENCE OF ANUJANMA NAKSHATRAS 54
CHAPTER 5: TRIJANMA NAKSHATRAS: THE LAST NAKSHATRA
GROUP 55
    DIFFERENT TYPES OF KARMA 63
    EFFECTS OF PLANETS IN VARIOUS HOUSES 64

PART THREE: LUNAR MANSIONS IN PREDICTIVE ASTROLOGY 66
CHAPTER 6: TIMING OF EVENTS: UDU-DASHAS 67
Understanding Udu Dasha 68
Vimshottari Dasha System and Nakshatras 69
Nakshatras and Planet Transits 72
CHAPTER 7: NAKSHATRAS AND RELATIONSHIP COMPATIBILITY 78
Ashtakoot Guna Milan 80
CHAPTER 8: NAKSHATRAS AND CAREER PLANNING 90
Ashwini - The Star of Transport 90
Bharani - The Star of Restraint 91
Krittika - The Star of Fire 92
Rohini - The Star of Ascent 92
Mrigashirsha - The Searching Star 93
Ardra - The Star of Sorrow 93
Punarvasu - The Star of Renewal 94
Pushya - The Star of Nourishment 94
Ashlesha - The Clinging Star 95
Magha - The Star of Power 95
Purva Phalguni - The Fruit of the Tree 96
Uttara Phalguni - The Star of Patronage 96
Hasta 97
Chitra - The Star of Opportunity 97
Swati - The Self-Motivated Star 98
Vishakha - The Star of Purpose 98
Anuradha - The Star of Success 99
Jyeshta - The Elder or Chief Star 100
Moola - The Foundation Star 100
Purvashada - The Invincible Star 101
Uttarashada - The Universal Star 101
Shravana - The Star of Learning 102
Dhanishta - The Star of Symphony 102
Shatabisha - The Hundred Stars 103
Purva Bhadrapada - The Burning Pair 103

Uttara Bhadrapada – the Warrior Star 104
Revati – the Wealthy Star 104
CHAPTER 9: THE MUHURTA: ELECTIONAL ASTROLOGY 106
Understanding the Concept of Muhurta 106
Selection of the Muhurta 108
The Thithi 109
Vara or Weekday 110
Timing of Events and 27 Nakshatras 111
How to Find an Auspicious Muhurta 114
CHAPTER 10: THE K.P. SYSTEM OF STELLAR ASTROLOGY 115
Deviations from Vedic Astrology 116
Basic Concepts of K. P. System 118
Significance of Sub-Lords in K. P. System 120
CONCLUSION 123
HERE'S ANOTHER BOOK BY MARI SILVA THAT YOU MIGHT LIKE 125
YOUR FREE GIFT (ONLY AVAILABLE FOR A LIMITED TIME) 126
RESOURCES 127

Introduction

Nakshatras are segments of the ecliptic through which the Moon passes on its orbit around the Earth. Otherwise known as lunar mansions, ancient cultures use them in their organization of the calendar. Simply put, Nakshatras are asterisms, constellations, or groups of stars that are fixed and immobile. Planets pass over them as they move in their orbits.

The ancient Indian sages who created the Vedic Astrology and Nakshatras system say these lunar mansions are the homes in which the fruits of labor—or karma, in Sanskrit—are stored. The stars of asterisms distribute karma in the present life.

Although more popular in Hindu Astrology, the concept of using stars of asterisms was adopted in other parts of the world, too, including the Euphrates Valley of Mesopotamia, Babylonia, Egypt, Arabia, and Person.

The history of the study of Nakshatras is not relevant in this book. More interesting is that by knowing about Nakshatras and their influences on your life, you can know where your life is going, and potentially, even find out why.

This comprehensive publication on Nakshatras extensively covers the basic aspects of this fascinating topic. While it may take years of learning and practice to master this idea, it has been written in simple, easy-to-understand language, and is great for beginners who want to test the waters.

The best part of the book is that it has all the latest trends in Nakshatras' realm, along with the updated tools used to arrive at predictions. The chapters have been arranged so you will learn the simplest topics first and develop into the progressively complex topics. It is best to start from the first topic to get an idea of each chapter before moving on to the next. By the time you finish the book, your understanding of Nakshatras and their effects on human life will have exceeded your original expectations.

PART ONE: The 27 Lunar Mansions

Chapter 1: Introduction to the 27 Lunar Mansions

Nakshatra is a Sanskrit term relating to a house (mansion) of the moon—astrologically referred to as a lunar mansion. The term Nakshatra is used both in Indian astronomy and in Hindu or Vedic Astrology. The moon's ecliptic orbit around the Earth is divided into 27 sectors, each of which is a Nakshatra. Each Nakshatra's name is connected to an important star or group of stars (asterism) in that sector.

According to Vedic Astrology, in Sanskrit, Nakshatra translates to "star," and the 27 Nakshatras play an undeniably important role in astrological calculations. As you may call it, the Zodiac—or the heavens—was categorized into twelve Rashis or Zodiac Signs. India's ancient seers used a more accurate and detailed categorization of the heavens into 27 Nakshatras or asterisms.

These 27 Nakshatras or constellations are about 300-400 light-years away from the Earth. Vedic Astrology offers detailed descriptions along with accurate mathematical and astronomical calculations by which a practitioner has a powerful predictive tool in their hand based on an individual's Nakshatra at their birth.

According to ancient Vedic astrology, the starting point of the 27 Nakshatras is "Kritika," or the vernal equinox's position. However, more recent compilations of Vedic Astrology take the starting point of the list of 27 Nakshatras as "Ashwini," a point on the ecliptic that is directly opposite to "Chitra," the Sanskrit name for the star Spica. "Ashwini" is the asterism connected to the modern constellation of Aries. The first Vedic Astrological text that lists these 27 Nakshatras is Vedanga Jyotisha.

The Hindu scriptures like the Mahabharata and Harivamsa credit the creation of the Nakshatras to Daksha, an important son of Lord Brahma, the universe's creator. The story of Daksha and how he is credited with creating the Nakshatra goes as follows:

Lord Brahma, the creator of the universe, created Daksha, Kamadeva, Dharma, and Agni from his right thumb, heart, chest, and eyebrows, respectively. Daksha is portrayed as a fat man with a protruding belly and an ibex's head with spiral horns. Daksha and his wife Prasuti had many daughters. He married 27 of them to Chandra, the Moon God.

Interestingly, Chandra was only keen on marrying one of Daksha's daughters, Rohini, but Daksha requested the Moon God to marry another 26, along with Rohini. Thus, the 27 wives of Chandra, the Moon God, became the 27 Nakshatras or Lunar Mansions.

In the Atharva Veda, one of the four Vedas in the Sanatana Dharma—now known in the Western world as Hinduism—talks about 28 Nakshatras, which are used as celestial markers in the sky. When these 28 stars were mapped into equal divisions of the ecliptic, it resulted in 27 divisions. Those represented 27 cleaner and more accurate segments, each subtending to 13° 20' (13 degrees 20 minutes) instead of 12° 5 1-3/7' (12 degrees and 1-3/7 minutes) in the earlier 28 sections.

The 27 stars according to Vedic Astrology are Ashwini, Bharani, Kritika, Rohini, Mrigashirsha, Ardra, Punarvasu, Pushya, Aslesha, Magha, Purva Phalguni, Uttara Phalguni, Hasta, Chitra, Swati,

Vishakha, Anuradha, Jyeshtha, Moola, Purvashada, Uttarashada, Shravana, Dhanishta, Satabhisha, Purva Bhadrapada, Uttara Bhadrapada, and Revati.

The Nakshatra Abhijit was left out from the 28 listed in the Atharva Veda; however, rare astrological schools consider all 28 Nakshatras. Interestingly, this abandoned Nakshatra Abhijit plays an important role while deciding auspicious times to conduct important events in all schools of Vedic Astrology.

Relationship Between Nakshatras and Zodiac Signs

Understanding planetary rulers form a key element in Vedic Astrology. In ancient Hindu Astrology, only the five visible planets, namely Mercury, Venus, Mars, Jupiter, and Saturn, along with the Sun and Moon, are the rulers of the twelve Zodiac Signs covering the 27 Nakshatras. These seven heavenly bodies together are referred to as the "Traditional Rulers." The Sun and Moon rule one Zodiac sign each—Leo and Cancer, respectively—and the remaining five visible planets rule two signs each. In addition to the Traditional Rulers, Rahu and Ketu (Lunar Nodes) also rule certain Nakshatras.

Another important point to note is that Zodiac signs also have their own lords, taken from the nine rulers described above. Every Nakshatra is ruled by its own lord and gets influenced by the lord of the sign to which it belongs.

The above 27 Nakshatras start at Ashwini at 0 degrees, and each of the Nakshatras covers 13 degrees, 20 minutes in 360 degrees of the path. Further, each of these Nakshatras is divided into four quarters (Padas) measuring 3 degrees, 20 minutes. The twelve Rashis covers 30 degrees each in the 360-degree path. The first Rashi or the Zodiac sign, namely Mesha—which covers 0-30 degrees—has ten padas of the first three Nakshatras as follows:

- All the four padas of the first Nakshatra, Ashwini (13 degrees, 20 minutes)
- All the four padas of the second Nakshatra, Bharani (13 degrees, 20 minutes)
- The first pada of the third Nakshatra, Kritika (3 degrees, 20 minutes)

So, the next Rashi, Vrishabh, will have the following Nakshatra padas covered in it:

- The second, third, and the fourth pada of third Nakshatra, Kritika (10 degrees)
- All the four padas of the fourth Nakshatra, Rohini (13 degrees, 20 minutes)
- The first and second padas of the fifth Nakshatra, Mrigasheersha (6 degrees, 40 minutes)

Like this, each of the twelve Rashis encloses nine padas from the various Nakshatras, taken in order.

Now, look at each of these Nakshatras in more detail.

The 27 Nakshatras

Ashwini - The Ashwini Nakshatra ranges from 0 degrees to 13 degrees, 20 minutes in the Mesha Rashi or the Aries sign. Ketu, the Serpent God, is the ruler of Ashwini Nakshatra. Ashwini is identified with the serpent god and also symbolizes all the serpentine qualities. Its symbol is the horse's head.

Bharani - The Bharani Nakshatra ranges between 13 degrees, 20 minutes, and 24 degrees, 40 minutes in the Mesha Rashi, or the Aries sign. The Lord Yama, the God of Death, is the ruler of the Bharani Nakshatra. Lord Yama is the dispenser of justice as he analyzes the good and bad actions and behaviors of a person, determining the punishment or reward for the person's soul after their death. The symbol of Bharani Nakshatra is the Yoni.

Kritika - The Kritika Nakshatra ranges from 26 degrees, 40 minutes from the Aries sign to 10 degrees in the Vrishabh Rashi or Taurus sign. The ruler of Kritika Nakshatra is the Sun God, Surya. People born in this Nakshatra are usually tenacious, determined, and have a strong will to get what they want. Its symbol is the razor.

Rohini - Rohini Nakshatra ranges from 10 degrees to 23 degrees, 20 minutes in the Vrishabh Rashi. The ruling planet of the Rohini Nakshatra is Chandra, the Moon. This star focuses on spiritual liberation and the idea that desiring anything that is not yours is not a good thing. It symbolizes a chariot and is also referred to as the "Red One." Its symbol is the chariot.

Mrigashirsha - The Mrigashirsha Nakshatra ranges from 23 degrees, 20 minutes in the Vrishabh Rashi to 6 degrees, 40 minutes in Mithuna Rashi, or Gemini Zodiac sign. Mrigashirsha translates to "deer's head" and symbolizes benevolence. The ruling planet is Mars, and its symbol is the deer's head.

Ardra - The Ardra Nakshatra ranges from 6 degrees, 40 minutes to 20 degrees in Mithuna Rashi. It is ruled by Lord Rudra, the manifestation of power and dominance, as well as Rahu, the shadow planet, which can bring many miseries, including sadness and poverty. Its symbol is a teardrop.

Punarvasu - Ranging from 20 degrees in Mithuna Rashi to 3 degrees, 20 minutes in Karka Rashi (the Cancer zodiac sign), Punarvasu means the return of light. The ruling planet is Jupiter, and people born under this Nakshatra are known for their never-give-up attitude. They can stand up and fight regardless of the number of times they are beaten. Its symbol is a quiver.

Pushya - The Pushya Nakshatra ranges from 3 degrees, 20 minutes to 16 degrees, 40 minutes in the Karka Rashi. The Lord of this Nakshatra is Saturn, and natives of Pushya are usually happy, rich, good-looking, stable-minded, and have self-esteem. Its symbol is the udder.

Aslesha - The Ashlesha Nakshatra ranges from 16 degrees, 40 minutes to 30 degrees in Karka Rashi, and is ruled by the Serpent God. Ashlesha translates to "Naga," or the serpent deity, and represents snake-like qualities such as entwining, embracing, and clinging. Its symbol is a serpent.

Magha - The Magha Nakshatra ranges from 0 degrees to 13 degrees, 20 minutes in the Simha Rashi (the Zodiac Sign of Leo). The natives born in Magha Nakshatra are usually attracted to occult sciences and are prone to invoking and praying to their ancestors. Ketu rules this Nakshatra, and its symbol is a throne.

Purva Phalguni - The Purva Phalguni Nakshatra ranges from 13 degrees, 20 minutes to 26 degrees, 40 minutes in the Simha Rashi, and is ruled by the planet Venus. Natives born in this Nakshatra usually love to enjoy materialistic comforts. Its symbol is a hammock.

Uttara Phalguni - The Uttara Phalguni Nakshatra ranges from 26 degrees, 40 minutes in the Simha Rashi to 10 degrees in Kanya Rashi (Virgo zodiac sign). The ruler of Uttara Phalguni is Surya, the Sun God. Natives born under this Nakshatra are usually friendly and independent. Its symbol is a fig tree.

Hasta - The Hasta Nakshatra ranges from 10 degrees to 23 degrees, 20 minutes in Kanya Rashi. The Lord of Hasta Nakshatra is Chandra, the Moon God. People born in this Nakshatra are typically pure in thought, word, and deed. Its symbol is the hand.

Chitra - The Chitra Nakshatra ranges from 23 degrees, 20 minutes in the Kanya Rashi, and goes up to 6 degrees, 40 minutes in Tula Rashi (Libra zodiac sign). The planet Mars rules the Chitra Nakshatra. Its symbol is a jewel.

Swati - Ranging from 6 degrees, 40 minutes to 20 degrees in Tula Rashi, Swati Nakshatra is ruled by Rahu, the shadow planet. People born in Swati Nakshatra are usually skilled at their profession, compassion, soft-spoken, and generous. Its symbol is coral.

Vishakha - The Vishakha Nakshatra ranges from 20 degrees in Tula Rashi to 3 degrees, 20 minutes in Vrischika Rashi (Scorpio). Ruled by the planet Jupiter, the natives born in Vishakha Nakshatra are usually adept at making money. Its symbol is an arch.

Anuradha - The Anuradha Nakshatra ranges from 3 degrees, 20 minutes to 16 degrees, 40 minutes in Vrischika Rashi. Interestingly, Vrischika Rashi is ruled by the aggressive planet Mars, and Saturn rules the Anuradha Nakshatra. Now, Mars and Saturn are considered rivals with characteristics that are starkly different from each other. So, people born in Anuradha Nakshatra demonstrate peculiar traits. Its symbol is a lotus.

Jyeshtha - The Jyeshtha Nakshatra ranges from 16 degrees, 40 minutes to 30 degrees in Vrischika Rashi. The ruling lord of this Nakshatra is the planet Mercury. People born under this Nakshatra have excellent analytical skills, are virtuous and cheerful, but have very few friends. Its symbol is an amulet.

Moola - The Moola Nakshatra ranges from 0 degrees to 13 degrees, 20 minutes in Dhanush Rashi (Sagittarius). The controlling planet of Moola is Ketu. Roots are the symbol of this constellation.

Purvashada - The Purvashada Nakshatra ranges from 13 degrees, 20 minutes to 26 degrees, 40 minutes in Dhanush Rashi. People born in this Nakshatra are usually very proud, compatible with their partners, and are attached to their friends. The ruling planet is planet Venus, and the symbol is a fan.

Uttarashada - The Uttarashada Nakshatra ranges from 13 degrees, 20 minutes in the Dhanush Rashi to 10 degrees in Makar Rashi (Capricorn). The ruling Lord of this Nakshatra is Surya or the Sun. People born in this Nakshatra are usually grateful, obedient, and spiritual seekers. Its symbol is the tusk.

Shravana - The Shravana Nakshatra ranges from 10 degrees to 23 degrees, 20 minutes in Makar Rashi. It is ruled by the Moon or Chandra. People born in this Nakshatra are usually seekers of knowledge and wisdom. Its symbol is an ear.

Dhanishta - Ruled by Mars, the Dhanishta Nakshatra ranges from 23 degrees, 20 minutes in Makar Rashi to 6 degrees, 40 minutes in Kumbha Rashi (Aquarius). The ruling god is Saturn. People born in this Nakshatra are usually versatile and intelligent. Its symbol is a drum.

Satabhisha - The Satabhisha Nakshatra ranges from 6 degrees, 40 minutes to 20 degrees in Kumbha Rashi. The ruling planet is Rahu. People born in this Nakshatra are truthful and honest, even though they talk harshly. Its symbol is a collection of 1,000 stars.

Purva Bhadrapada - The Purva Bhadrapada Nakshatra ranges from 20 degrees in Kumbha Rashi to 3 degrees, 20 minutes in Meena Rashi (Pisces). The ruling planet is Jupiter. People born in this Nakshatra are usually intelligent and adept at making money. Its symbol is a funeral cot.

Uttara Bhadrapada - Ranging from 3 degrees, 20 minutes to 16 degrees, 40 minutes in Meena Rashi, the Uttara Bhadrapada Nakshatra is ruled by Saturn. People born under this Nakshatra are usually happy, love children, and have good oratory skills. Its symbol is a water snake.

Revati - The Revati Nakshatra ranges from 16 degrees, 40 minutes to 30 degrees in Meena Rashi. The ruling planet is Mercury. People born under this Nakshatra are usually amicable, knowledgeable, and wealthy. Its symbol is a fish.

Categorizations of the 27 Nakshatras

The 27 Nakshatras are categorized into different types based on their favorability for auspicious times of various events.

Sthira or Fixed - There are four Nakshatras, namely Rohini, Uttara Phalguni, Uttara Ashadha, and Uttara Bhadrapada, referred to as fixed or sthira. Sthira translates to stable, and so, these asterisms are excellent for activities with long-term effects and outcomes, such as tree planting, buying a home or other property, and construction of buildings.

Ugra or Fierce - The five constellations classified as fierce or ugra are Bharani, Magha, Purva Phalguni, Purva Ashadha, and Purva Bhadrapada. According to Hindu Astrology, these asterisms are excellent for activities involving fire, destruction, demolitions, weapons, handling of excessive force, confronting enemies and rivals, etc.

Chara or Movable - The five asterisms categorized as movable are Punarvasu, Swati, Shravana, Dhanishtha, and Shatabhisha. Chara translates to movability, and so these Nakshatras are ideal for activities connected to mobility and moving parts and items. Examples include the purchase of vehicles, going on journeys, or traveling.

Mridu or Tender - The four Nakshatras categorized as tender or mridu are Mrigashira, Chitra, Anuradha, and Revati. Due to their tender nature, these asterisms are suitable for seeking and enjoying pleasures and pleasurable activities. For example, they are good for writing poetry, making new friends, the beginnings of dramas, and dances.

Tikshna or Sharp - Four Nakshatras are categorized as sharp or tikshna, including Ardra, Ashlesha, Jyeshtha, and Mula. These asterisms' sharp nature renders them useful for difficult activities such as filing for divorce, black magic, casting spells, exorcism, and hypnotism.

Kshipra or Swift - There are three asterisms categorized as Kshipra or swift, namely Ashwini, Pushya, and Hasta. Their swift nature makes these Nakshatras highly suitable for finance, education, and trade-related activities. Thus, these constellations are suitable for trade and commerce transactions, admission to institutions, loan-related tasks, taking medication, and journey and travel.

Misra or Mixed - Two Nakshatras, namely Krittika and Vishaka, are called mixed or misra. Due to their mixed nature, these asterisms are good for routine activities such as worshipping, purchasing electronics and furniture, and fire ceremonies.

Chapter 2: A Closer Look at Nakshatras

Chapter 1 provided basic information about each Nakshatra. Chapter 2 takes a closer look at each of the 27 Nakshatras. However, before that, there are other preliminary and very important elements in Vedic Astrology that you need to be aware of.

The Three Gunas

Indian philosophy divides reality into two categories: Purusha, the knower, and Prakriti, the known. Purusha or the Self is never an experiential object; it is always the subject matter. Purusha is that which knows everything and is totally aware. On the other hand, Prakriti is all that shows itself, including material and psychological elements. Prakriti consists of everything that can be known.

Prakriti is a gigantic reservoir of limitless potential or energy made up of three primary forces or gunas, which include Sattva, Rajas, and Tamas. Each of these gunas has its own characteristics. Knowing how these three gunas work and understanding their essence is an important tool on the spiritual path. It also plays an important role in Vedic Astrology. Now, look at each of these three gunas—which translates to "strand" or "fiber"—in more detail.

Sattva - Sattva behaves like a transparent glass, allowing the light and knowledge of the pure consciousness to flow through easily. It has the power to unveil the ultimate truth—or Sat in Sanskrit. Sattva manifests through inspiration, beauty, and balance and promotes health, contentment, and energy. Sattva is the energy connected to liberation. It goes beyond the materialistic world and yearns to return to its original, heavenly abode.

Rajas - This fundamental force of Prakriti is related to change and is characterized by passion, effort, desire, and pain. The activity of Rajas can drive you toward Sattva (increased spirituality) or Tamas (increased desire for materialism). Although it can have positive or negative outcomes, Rajas is characterized by unsteadiness, agitation, and unhappiness.

Tamas - This fundamental force or energy layer of Prakriti hides the presence of Pure Consciousness. The power of Tamas to obscure results in dullness and ignorance. This fundamental force is heavy and dense. Interestingly, another synonym of Tamas is "sthithi," or being steady. Tamas, in a Sattvic form, can have a steadying influence in one's life. For example, resting during illness can be therapeutic.

Tamas is almost always characterized by immobilization. Therefore, tamasic foods are impure, stale, and lifeless. Tamasic entertainment is intoxicating and mindless. All things from Tamas invariably leads to inaction even when action is the need of the hour. The attraction to lethargy, sleep, and procrastination is a common tamasic effect that nearly everyone experiences. Tamas is all about the material world.

Nakshatras and the Three Gunas

Each of the 27 Nakshatras represents the three gunas in three different ways or levels. Now, look at each of the three levels to understand the connection between gunas and Nakshatras better.

First-Level Relationship - The 27 Nakshatras are divided into three categories, each with nine Nakshatras representing one of the three fundamental forces. Thus, at a primary level:

- Nine of the 27 Nakshatras representing Rajas energy coincide with the Zodiac Signs Aries, Taurus, Gemini, and Cancer.

- Another group of nine Nakshatras representing Tamas energy coincides with the Zodiac Signs Leo, Virgo, Libra, and Scorpio.

- The third group of nine Nakshatras representing Sattva energy coincides with the Zodiac signs Sagittarius, Capricorn, Aquarius, and Pisces.

Second-Level Relationship - Each group of nine Nakshatras is further divided into three groups of three Nakshatras, each at the secondary level. So, the nine Nakshatras representing Rajas energy at the primary level are divided as follows:

- The first three Nakshatras represent Rajas at the secondary level.
- The next three represent Tamas at the secondary level.
- The last three represent Sattva at the secondary level.

Similarly, the nine Nakshatras representing Tamas energy are divided into three groups as follows at the secondary level:

- The first three Nakshatras represent Rajas energy.
- The second three Nakshatras represent Tamas energy.
- The last three Nakshatras represent Sattva energy.

In the same way, the nine Nakshatras representing Sattva energy are divided into three groups as follows:
- The first three Nakshatras represent Rajas energy.
- The second three Nakshatras represent Tamas energy.
- The last three Nakshatras represent Sattva energy.

Tertiary-Level Relationship - Each of the three Nakshatras at the secondary level is further divided into three categories, each representing Rajas, Tamas, and Sattva energies. With this system, the 27 Nakshatras and the three fundamental energies interacting with each other along with their respective planetary lords are as follows:

1. Ashwini - Rajas-Rajas-Rajas - Ketu
2. Bharani - Rajas-Rajas-Tamas - Venus (or Shukra)
3. Krittika - Rajas-Rajas-Sattva - Sun (Surya)
4. Rohini - Rajas-Tamas-Rajas - Moon (Chandra)
5. Mrigashirsha - Rajas-Tamas-Tamas - Mars (Guja)
6. Ardra - Rajas-Tamas-Sattva - Rahu
7. Punarvasu - Rajas-Sattva-Rajas - Jupiter (Guru)
8. Pushya - Rajas-Sattva-Tamas - Saturn (Shani)
9. Ashlesha - Rajas-Sattva-Sattva - Mercury (Bhuddh)
10. Magha - Tamas-Rajas-Rajas - Ketu
11. Purva Phalguni - Tamas-Rajas-Tamas - Venus (Shukra)
12. Uttara Phalguni - Tamas-Rajas-Sattva - Sun (Surya)
13. Hasta - Tamas-Tamas-Rajas - Moon (Chandra)
14. Chitra - Tamas-Tamas-Tamas - Mars (Guja)
15. Swati - Tamas-Tamas-Sattva - Rahu
16. Vishakha - Tamas-Sattva-Rajas - Jupiter (Guru)
17. Anuradha - Tamas-Sattva-Tamas - Saturn (Shani)

18. Jyeshta – Tamas-Sattva-Sattva – Mercury (Buddh)

19. Mula – Sattva-Rajas-Rajas – Ketu

20. Purvashadha – Sattva-Rajas-Tamas – Venus (Shukra)

21. Uttarashadha – Sattva-Rajas-Sattva – Sun (Surya)

22. Shravana – Sattva-Tamas-Rajas – Moon (Chandra)

23. Dhanistha – Sattva-Tamas-Tamas – Mars (Guja)

24. Shatabhisha – Sattva-Tamas-Sattva – Rahu

25. Purva Bhadrapada – Sattva-Sattva-Rajas – Jupiter (Guru)

26. Uttara Bhadrapada – Sattva-Sattva-Tamas – Saturn (Shani)

27. Revati – Sattva-Sattva-Sattva – Mercury (Bhuddh)

Connection Between Lords of the Nakshatras and the Gunas

The lords of the Nakshatras play an important role in the life of a person. The lord of the Nakshatra, in which the Moon is placed at the time of a person's birth, determines the first "dasa" of the individual's life. Dasas and their importance will be detailed later. Interestingly, a critical connection can be found between the lords of the Nakshatras and the gunas.

- Ketu, Shukra, and Surya are the lords of those Nakshatras with Rajas at the secondary level.

- Chandra, Guja, and Rahu are the lords of the Nakshatras with Tamas at the secondary level.

- Guru, Shani, and Bhuddh are the lords of the Nakshatras with Sattva at the secondary level.

Now, look at the tertiary level.

- Shukra, Guja, and Shani are the lords of the Nakshatras that have Tamas at the tertiary level.
- Surya, Rahu, and Bhuddh are the Nakshatras lords with Sattva at the tertiary level.
- Ketu, Chandra, and Guru are the lords of those Nakshatras that have Rajas at the tertiary level.

Looking at the secondary and tertiary levels, you get the following information about the nine planets and the gunas.

- Ketu – Rajas-Rajas
- Shukra (Venus) – Rajas-Tamas
- Surya (Sun) – Rajas-Sattva
- Chandra (Moon) – Tamas-Rajas
- Guja (Mars) – Tamas-Tamas
- Rahu – Tamas-Sattva
- Guru (Jupiter) – Sattva-Rajas
- Shani (Saturn) – Sattva-Tamas
- Bhuddh (Mercury) – Sattva-Sattva

Now, you can draw some really fascinating connections between the planets and the gunas with examples.

- Venus (Shukra) is known for love and lust. To get love and lust, you take action (Rajas), and the deeper you get into action, the more you fall into ignorance (Tamas).
- Surya is a fiery (Rajas) planet, but it also represents the soul and has Sattva characteristics.
- Guru is also a fiery (Rajas) planet. However, again, Guru represents inner wisdom and is Sattvic.

- Saturn is a spiritual (Sattva) planet because it is related to Sannyas (renouncement). But Saturn also represents matter (or material), which is why it has Tamasic characteristics.

- Rahu is like Shani but in the reverse order. Rahu takes you so deep into materialistic life that you accept everything that this life has to give you and then follow the path of liberation (Sattva).

- Bhuddh (Mercury) comes across as the most spiritual planet—and the reason is clear. It is an airy planet and has the power to liberate you from suffering. Unlike animals, human beings can think for themselves. Mercury helps you do that. It is neither connected to Tamas (materialism) nor Rajas (activity). It merely thinks about these two without going into either of the two.

Padas and Navamsas

As you already know, every Nakshatra is divided into four padas of 3 degrees, 30 minutes each. A Navamsa chart is used to depict the padas of Nakshatras. Nav-amsa means the "nine parts" or divisions of a Zodiac Sign. Each Zodiac sign has nine padas in it, making it a total of 108 padas in the entire elliptic. A Navamsa chart is considered the most important divisional charts—or Varga charts—to make predictive readings of an individual's life.

It has to be read in conjunction with the fundamental natal—or Rashi—chart. If the natal chart is compared to a blueprint, the Navamsa chart shows what that blueprint can become. Every pada is expressed through one of the twelve Navamsa signs and the ruling lord of that particular sign. Every pada alternates with male and female expressions, as do the twelve Zodiac Signs. Padas are discussed further in the next chapter.

The 27 Nakshatras and their Dileanations

Now, look at each of the 27 Nakshatras in more detail.

Ashwini - The Ashwini Nakshatra represents the Ashwini Kumara twins named Castor and Pullox. Spanning from 0 degrees to13 degrees, 20 minutes in Aries or Mesha Rashi, Ashwini's ruling planet is Ketu. The element connected to Ashwini is earth, and its symbol is the head of a horse.

The Ashwini Kumaras, the physicians to the gods or devas, rule over this constellation. This constellation can help people be free of diseases and deliver miraculous cures. People born in this Nakshatra are usually popular, good-looking, skillful, intelligent, and love all decorative elements.

The character of Ashwini Nakshatra is light and swift and is good for undertaking journeys, starting treatments, beginning a study course, making and manufacturing jewelry, and enjoying luxurious items.

Bharani - The ruler of Bharani is Lord Yama, the god of death, who has the power to take things away—referred to as apabharani shakti. So, Bharani Nakshatra takes away those things that have completed their life term on Earth and moves them to the next world. Lord Yama takes the soul of the person who has completed their life on Earth and takes it to the astral plane, where the soul can experience the effects of its karma of the present world and prepare itself for the next world or birth.

Lord Yama stands for discipline, sacrifice, cleanliness, purity, integrity, and justice. The Nakshatra, over which this lord rules also, is a giver of what is good, truthful, pure, and honest. Bharani Nakshatra's astrological nature is fierce and cruel. It is suitable for getting jobs done immediately, competitions, cruel deeds, and tasks related to poison, fire, and dangerous chemicals. Bharani Nakshatra is not suitable to start any auspicious events or work.

Bharani is connected to the earth element, and Shukra is the ruler of this constellation. Natives of Bharani Nakshatra are usually successful in their professions, truthful, and are free from grief. They will have a resolute character and no health issues.

Krittika – The first pada falls in Mesha Rashi while the remaining three padas fall in the Vrishabha Rashi. The ruling lord of Krittika is Agni, and the ruling planet is Surya. The element of Krittika is the earth, and the symbol is a goat. People born in the Krittika Nakshatra are usually attractive, voracious eaters, famous, and known to have a roving eye.

The lord of this Nakshatra is Agni, who has the power to burn, referred to as dahana shakti. The nature of Agni is to give light and heat, which are important elements for purification. So, the power of Krittika Nakshatra can burn up negativity, purifies a mixture of positive and negative, and can cook or ripen uncooked and raw things.

Krittika Nakshatra's nature is of mixed quality. It is an auspicious star for doing immediate actions, to start competitions, to work with metals, and to start an argument, but it is not an auspicious star to begin long-term, important tasks.

Rohini – All the four padas of Rohini Nakshatra are in Vrishabha Rashi. Derived from the Sanskrit root, Rohan meaning rising or coming into existence, Rohini is the birth star of Lord Krishna. According to Hindu mythology, Rohini was one of Chandra's 27 wives, the one he loved the most. Chandra rules Rohini, and the symbol is a cow-drawn cart.

Natives of Rohini Nakshatra are usually truthful, do not covet others' properties, speak sweetly, have clean habits, good-looking, and have firm views. The lord of Rohini Nakshatra is Lord Brahma, the creator, whose power is to create or grow, referred to as rohana shakti. Rohini Nakshatra's power lies in its ability to make anything fertile and allow for growth and development.

People born in Rohini Nakshatra—who invariably live well and abundantly—are also prone to jealous attacks from others. Yet, these are only side effects of the power of achieving great prosperity.

Being a steady and fixed Nakshatra, Rohini is auspicious for laying the foundations for cities, towns, digging wells, planting trees, coronations, building temples, installing deities, and other such activities that have lasting effects.

Mrigashirsha - The first and second padas of Mrigashirsha is in Vrishabha Rashi, and the third and fourth padas are in Mithuna Rashi. The ruling planet of this Nakshatra is Mangala or Mars, and the ruling lord is Chandra. The symbol of Mrigashirsha is the antelope.

People born in Mrigashirsha Nakshatra are usually skillful, good speakers, knowledgeable, and rich, but also cowardly and capricious. They are quite timid and peace-loving. The lord of Mrigashirsha is Chandra, also called Soma—the nectar of immortality)—the Moon God. Soma renders prana Shakti—or fulfillment. Chandra in Mrigashirsha also stands for weaving and expansion. So, Mrigashirsha Nakshatra has the power to fill their lives and those of others with joy and fulfillment.

Mrigashirsa is an auspicious star for accepting initiation, weddings, building constructions, and undertaking journeys. It has a gentle and soft nature and is good for learning arts, sensual pleasures, wearing new clothes, festivities, and other joyful events.

Ardra - All the four padas of Ardra Nakshatra are in Mithuna Rashi. The ruling lord of this Nakshatra is Rudra—a form of Lord Shiva—the trident and bow wielder. Ardra is the Janma Nakshatra of Lord Shiva. The ruling planet is Rahu, and the symbol is a teardrop.

Natives born under the Ardra Nakshatra are typically skillful traders and are highly interested in Tantric rituals. On the flip side, these natives can be quite ungrateful, have a fierce temper, and indulge in wicked deeds.

Lord Rudra represents thunder and is the fiercest form of Lord Shiva. His power lies in putting effort—yatna Shakti—into making gains in life. Hunting, searching, and achieving goals are the basis of yatna shakti. Ardra Nakshatra calls upon one to work hard and persistently to achieve their goals.

The Ardra Nakshatra is good if you need to fight off rivals and enemies, start tasks associated with fire, and for ghost hunting. Considering the fiercely destructible nature of Ardra Nakshatra, it is highly suitable for warfares, to invoke elemental spirits, and for acts of destruction.

Punarvasu - The first three padas of Punarvasu is in Mithuna Rashi, and the last pada is in Karkata Rashi. The ruling of this Nakshatra is Aditi, the Mother Goddess or the devas' mother, and the ruling planet is Guru (Jupiter). The element connected to Punarvasu is water.

People born in this constellation are typically morally and religiously good but can be quite dull and sickly. It would be easy to please people born in this Nakshatra with even small gifts. They are usually a fast walker.

Punarvasu is ruled by the Mother Goddess, known for Her power to gain materialistic wealth and prosperity—referred to as vasutva prapana shakti. She grants abundance to the earth and combines the power of rain or water and air or wind. So, this Nakshatra is great for revitalizing plant life. The power of Punarvasu renews and revitalizes creativity.

Pushya - All the four padas of Pushya Nakshatra are in Karkata Rashi (Cancer). Its ruling planet is Shani, and the ruling lord is Brihaspati, the guru of the devas. It is related to the water element, and the symbol is a cow's teat. Pushya translates to mean nourish, preserve, protect, multiple, strengthen, and replenish. Goddess Lakshmi and Goddess Sita are Pushya Nakshatra natives. People born in Pushya Nakshatra are usually learned, popular, rich, charitable, have control over their passions, adventurous, and lustful. They could be short.

The lord of Pushya Nakshatra is Brihaspati, who is believed to be the god of divine wisdom. He can create spiritual energy—referred to as brahmavarchas shakti. He stands for worshippers and sacrificial worship, both of which are important elements for creating spiritual energy.

He is also the lord of speech, specifically prayer, and all forms of worship, including meditation. Pushya Nakshatra enhances good karma and the outcomes of hard work. This Nakshatra is extremely auspicious to start religious and spiritual practices.

Ashlesha - All the four padas of Ashlesha Nakshatra are in Karkata Rashi. The twin brothers, Lakshman and Shatrughna in Valmiki Ramayana, were natives of this Nakshatra. The ruling planet is Mercury, and the element connected to it is water. The symbol of Ashlesha Nakshatra is a coiled snake.

People born in Aslesha Nakshatra can turn out to be cruel and ungrateful. They pay little attention to the work of other people and can be addicted to various vices. The ruling deity of this Nakshatra is the serpent god who can inflict poison (visasleshana shakti). The serpent god is also connected to trembling and agitation, and these powers can destroy victims.

While this power is good to drop harmful enemies, it can make the natives highly temperamental. Interestingly, serpents are also connected with using practical wisdom, through which one can overcome enemies and other obstacles in their life path.

Magha - All the four padas of Magha Nakshatra are in Simha Rashi (Leo Zodiac). Its ruling planet is Ketu, and its ruling deity is "pitrugan." The symbol of Magha Nakshatra is a royal court with a throne. It is associated with the water element.

People born in Magha Nakshatra are usually wealthy and have many servants to do their bidding. They respect elders and gods and are also very enterprising. Ruled by the "pitrugan" or ancestors, this Nakshatra reflects the power of leaving or giving up one's body—referred to as tyage kshepani shakti. It also represents mourning. Both these characteristic features stand for death or the end of a particular cycle.

Magha Nakshatra is like Bharani Nakshatra, as the latter also represents the soul's movement away from one's body. Another meaning of Magha Nakshatra is related to ancestors and one's pride in ancestral legacy.

This constellation has a cruel and fierce nature and is suitable to undertake tasks related to conflict, deceit, destroying one's enemies, battling and fighting, and other unkind acts. Magha Nakshatra is unsuitable for the start of auspicious activities.

Purva Phalguni - All the four padas of Purva Phalguni Nakshatra are in Simha Rashi. Its ruling planet is Venus, and the ruling deity is Lord Shiva in his Shivalinga form. The symbol of Purva Phalguni is a swinging hammock and is connected with the water element. Goddess Kamakshi or Sri Lalita Tripura Sundari are born in this Nakshatra. It is also the birth star of Guru or Jupiter.

People born in Purva Phalguni Nakshatra are usually fond of traveling—they are wanderers—talk well, loyal, and are good-looking. According to Taittiriya Brahmanas, Purva Phalguni is ruled by Aryaman, the God of unions and contracts, who has the power of procreation—referred to as prajanana shakti. The other qualities of this Nakshatra are those connected with female and male partners.

These powers of Purva Phalguni stand for the union and procreations at all levels of human life, but as Aryaman is the ruler of productive alliances, Purva Phalguni union and procreating powers have approved social and familial agreements.

Uttara Phalguni - The first pada of Uttara Phalguni is in Simha Rashi, and the remaining three padas are in Kanya Rashi. The ruling planet is Surya, and the ruling deity is Aryaman—although Taittiriya Brahmana says that the ruling deity of Uttara Phalguni is Bhaga, the god of happiness. The symbol of this constellation is a bed, and it is associated with the fire element.

People born in Uttara Phalguni are usually happy, popular, and make their own wealth and property. They have the power to subdue their enemies and enjoy all the pleasures of life, including being versed in the arts, association with women, and more.

Bhaga, the god of happiness, is related to the power of accumulating prosperity—referred to as chayani shakti—through unions and marriages. Bhaga's power deals with wealth accumulated from one's own family and wealth derived from the partner's family. So, Uttara Phalguni represents prosperity through unions and marriages.

Hasta - All the four padas are in Kanya Rashi (Virgo Zodiac). Its ruling deity is Surya, and its symbol is a closed hand. It is associated with the fire element. People born in Hasta Nakshatra are usually intelligent, enterprising, enthusiastic, and will serve others, but they can also be thieves, drunkards, and cruel.

According to Taittiriya Brahmana, Hasta Nakshatra is ruled by Savitar, the creative aspect of Surya, the Sun God, who has the power to help one gain what they seek and place it in their hands—referred to as hasta sthapaniya agama shakti. The pursuit of Hasta Nakshatra natives is to seek gains and work toward making the gains. Hasta Nakshatra facilitates the successful and immediate achievement of goals.

Hasta is a swift or light constellation and is good for enjoying luxury items, sports activities and exercises, starting art industries, medical treatments, seeing friends, and fine arts. It is also good for receiving and giving loans.

Chitra – The first two padas of Chitra Nakshatra are in Kanya Rashi, and the last two padas are in Tula Rashi. The ruling planet is Mars or Mangala, and the ruling deity is Vishwakarma, the architect of the gods. Its symbol is the gem found on the serpent's crest.

People born in Chitra Nakshatra love clothes, flowers, and garlands. They are good-looking and kindhearted. They are learned, wealthy, enjoy the pleasures of life, and can be scholarly.

Vishwakarma is known as the cosmic craftsman. The power of Chitra Nakshatra is its ability to accumulate good deeds—referred to as punya chayani shakti. It is also connected with law and truth. These three qualities help people born in Chitra Nakshatra to gain honor in their work or profession.

Chitra Nakshatra allows one to gain the fruit of righteous good deeds. This constellation has a powerful spiritual effect. It is a gentle and soft-natured Nakshatra and is good for making friends, learning fine arts, decorations, and starting auspicious events.

Swati – All the four padas of Swati Nakshatra are in Tula Rashi. The ruling planet is Rahu, its ruling deity is Vayu, the wind god, and its symbol is the buffalo. People born in Swati Nakshatra are usually quiet and mild-mannered. They are skilled in their trade and have great control over their passions.

They are expert orators and can rise to become famous in their area of expertise. They are highly self-restrained and educated. The ruling deity of Swati Nakshatra is Vayu, the God of Wind, who has the power to scatter things (pradhvamsa shakti). Swati Nakshatra is connected with changing forms and moving in various directions. So, this constellation represents transformation.

Vishakha – The first three padas are in the Kanya Rashi, and the fourth pada is in the Vrischika Rashi (Scorpio Zodiac). The ruling planet of Vishakha Nakshatra is Jupiter or Guru, and its ruling deity is Satragni—also known as Indragni. Its symbol is a triumphal gate decked with green leaves.

Vishakha Nakshatra is also called Radha, as it is believed to be complementary to Anuradha Nakshatra. Lord Subramanya or Lord Muruga is born in the Vishakha Nakshatra. Other important people born in this Nakshatra are Lord Buddha, Napoleon, and the Sun God, Surya.

People born in the Vishakha Nakshatra are typically good speakers, good-looking, make a lot of money but also are greedy and jealous. Natives born in this Nakshatra have the power to win over their senses. They are wealthy and miserly.

Vishakha is ruled by Agni and Indra (Indragni). Both these gods together represent the power of heat and light in the atmosphere resulting in the successful fruition of their labors—this power is referred to as vyapana shakti. The star also represents the power of plowing and harvest, which helps one achieve the fruits of their labor, even if these fruits take time to obtain.

Anuradha - All the four padas of Anuradha Nakshatra are in Vrischika Rashi. Its ruling planet is Shani or Saturn, and its symbol is the same as Vishakha Nakshatra, leaf-decked triumphal gates. People born in Anuradha Nakshatra are usually fond of traveling, and many of them are destined to live in foreign countries.

The ruling deity of Anuradha Nakshatra is Mitra, the divine ally with the power of worship—known as aradhana shakti. Mitra is also linked to the right relationships, compassion, and devotion. This constellation is connected to ascension and descension too. All these elements are meant for gaining honor and abundance. Goddess Lakshmi, the goddess of wealth, is of Anuradha Nakshatra.

People born in Anuradha Nakshatra seek balance in their relationships. They give respect and honor as much as they seek the same elements from their partners and friends.

Jyeshtha - All the four padas of Jyeshtha Nakshatra are in Vrischika Rashi. Its ruling planet is Bhuddh or Mercury, and its ruling deity is Lord Indra. The symbol is an earring or a circular talisman that is believed to represent Vishnu's disc's power. The animal symbol of Jyeshtha Nakshatra is a male hare or male deer. Lord Hayagriva, an incarnation of Lord Vishnu, is a native of Jyeshtha Nakshatra.

People born in this constellation are typically charitable, contented, wealthy, and have the power to endure much grief, but they can also be very irritable, have the power to curse others, and be cruel liars.

The ruling deity of Jyeshtha is Lord Indra, the king of devas or gods, who has the power to gain courage in battle and conquer his enemies—referred to as arohana shakti. Jyeshtha Nakshatra also represents the power to attack and defend. All these representations of power are related to heroism.

While Jyeshtha Nakshatra allows one to reach the pinnacle of personal power, it also calls for a lot of courage and effort to do so. This constellation shows that everyone has to win their karmic battles through the effective use of energies and mental powers, and not necessarily through the strength of arms and weapons.

Moola - All the four padas are in Dhanush Rashi (Sagittarius Zodiac). Its ruling planet is Ketu, and its symbol is a cluster of roots. Its ruling deity is Alakshmi or Niritti. The meaning of Moola Nakshatra is also "reverse" or "opposite."

People born in Moola Nakshatra are usually rich, happy, steady, and have a good life, but they can also be liars and trouble others. Niritti or Alakshmi is the goddess of destruction who has the power to destroy and bring about ruin (called barhana shakti). Moola Nakshatra stands for crushing and breaking things.

Moola Nakshatra reflects the importance of destruction in the continuous process of creation. Niritti also stands for Kali or the negative effects of time, which one has to accept as inevitable and use to their advantage.

Purvashadha - All the four padas of Purvashadha are in Dhanush Rashi. Its ruling planet is Venus or Shukra. Its ruling deity is Lord Varuna, the god of water, and its symbol is a hand fan. People born in Purvashadha usually make steady and firm friendships and will get loving spouses.

The power of Varuna, the ruling planet of Purvashada, is the power of invigoration—referred to as varchograhana shakti. This constellation is also connected with strength and relationships or connections. All of these powers are crucial to gain luster in life.

Purvashadha is all about regeneration and purification, like the purifying properties of water. Purification provides one with enhanced energy to strive for goals.

Uttarashadha - The first pada of Uttarashadha Nakshatra is in Dhanush Rashi, and the remaining three padas are in Makar Rashi (Capricorn Zodiac). The ruling planet is Surya, the Sun. The four planks of a bed are its symbol. Lord Ganesh is a native of Uttarashadha.

People born in this constellation are typically polite, virtuous, righteous, and have an attitude of gratitude. The ruling deity of Uttarashadha is Vishwe Deva (or the universal gods), whose power lies in the ability to grant unchallengeable wins and victories. This constellation represents the power to win and the insight of a winnable goal. So, Uttarashadha Nakshatra stands for unchallengeable victories.

Shravana - All the four padas of Shravana Nakshatra are in Makar Rashi. Its ruling planet is Chandra (Moon), and three footprints form its symbol. Its ruling deity is Lord Hari, a form of Vishnu. Shravana Nakshatra is the birth star of Lord Tirupati, Lord Vishnu, and Vamana, the fourth incarnation of the ten avatars of Lord Vishnu.

People born in Shravana Nakshatra are typically learned, liberal, and rich. They will get illustrious spouses toward whom the natives of Shravana Nakshatra will also be loving and affectionate.

Lord Hari, its ruling deity, is known for the power of connection—referred to as samhanana shakti. He is also related to seeking and paths of seeking. These powers together are important elements in building connections. Shravana can link people by connecting their life paths. Vamana, the fourth incarnation of Lord Vishnu, used three strides to connect the three worlds.

Dhanishta - The first two padas of Dhanishta are in Makar Rashi, and the second two padas are in Kumbha Rashi. Its ruling planet is Mars or Mangala, and its ruling deity is Asthavasu. People born in Dhanishta Nakshatra are usually courageous, rich, liberal, and fond of wealth and music. They could also be addicted to vices.

This constellation is ruled by Ashtavasu or the Vasus, who are known for their abundance. The power of the Vasus is connected to abundance and fame—referred to as khyapayitri shakti. Their power is also linked to birth and prosperity. These three powers help in bringing together the resources of different people to work as a team.

The Vasus are the deities of the earth and give abundant gifts to the earthly plane. They also manifest Agni or the sacred fire.

Shatabhistha - All the four padas of Shatabhistha are in Kumbha Rashi. Its ruling planet is Rahu, the symbol is a circle, and its ruling deity is Varuna, the god of water. People born in Shatabhistha Nakshatra are usually truthful and speak plainly. They are quite adventurous, too, but they could be afflicted by suffering from women in their lives. They own large homes and face the ups and downs of life heroically.

Varuna, the god of water, is the ruling deity of Shatabhistha, and he is known for his healing powers (bheshaja shakti). His power also stands for extension, pervasion, and support, all of which help free the world of calamity.

This constellation stands for the power to counter the suffering of difficult karma through repentance and divine grace. The healing powers of Shatabhistha lead to the revitalization of energy.

Purvabhadra - The first three padas are in Kumbha Rashi, and the last pada is in Meena Rashi. The ruling planet is Guru or Jupiter, its symbol is a double-faced man, and its ruling deity is Ajopada, a form of Lord Rudra or Shiva.

People born in Purvabhadra Nakshatra are usually skillful and heroic, but they are likely to face losses and calamities through women, be sorrowful due to the absence of a loved one, and be impatient.

This constellation is ruled by Ajopada or Aja Ekapad, the one-legged serpent, whose power lies in his ability to fire up an individual to achieve spiritual upliftment—referred to as yajamana udyamana shakti. This power is also related to what is good for the people and what is good for the gods. These three elements of this powerful constellation help support the universe, thereby removing the selfishness in people's lives and enhancing their spiritual power.

Uttarabhadra - All the four padas are in Kumbha Rashi. The ruling planet of Uttarabhadra Nakshatra is Shani or Saturn, its ruling deity is Ahirbudhyana, and its symbol is a serpent-like element.

People born in Uttarabhadra Nakshatra are typically witty speakers, morally good, happy, and tend to have many children and grandchildren. The ruling deity Ahirbhudyana is a serpent living in the atmosphere's depths, and its power lies in bringing rain to the earth.

The power of Ahirbhudyana also represents clouds above and the growth of plants below. These three powers represent stability on Earth. This constellation provides growth and prosperity in ways that help the entire world.

Revati - All the four padas of Revati Nakshatra are in Meena Rashi. The ruling planet is Bhuddh or Mercury, and its ruling deity is Pusan, who is the keeper of cows of the gods. Revati is the birth star of Shani.

People born in Revati Nakshatra are usually wealthy, courageous, clean, and have well-developed organs. They are scholarly and charming. Pusan, the ruling deity of Revati Nakshatra, is the Sun God's nourishing aspect, Surya. Its nourishment is symbolized by milk (kshiradyapani shakti).

The power of Pusan also stands for cows and calves. Milk, cows, and calves stand for world nourishment. So, Revati Nakshatra creates abundance and prosperity through nourishment. Pusan is the lord of cattle and the lord of paths. He stands for leading, protecting, and gathering (or herding) people together.

So, now that you have a general idea of Nakshatras through the detailed descriptions of all 27 of them, along with their significance, their ruling deities and planets, and their relationship with the three Gunas, you can move on to learning about Janma Nakshatras in the next chapter.

PART TWO: The Lunar Mansions Trilogy

Chapter 3: Janma Nakshatras: The First Nine Nakshatras

Now it is time to look a little deeper into the concept of padas before learning more about Nakshatras. As you already know, each Nakshatra has four padas. The four padas stand for four elements, namely:

- The first pada is Agni because it is mapped to Agni Navamsa
- The second pada is Prithvi – mapped to Prithvi Navamsa
- The third pada is Vayu
- The fourth pada is Jala

These padas also represent Dharma (Agni), Artha (Prithvi), Kama (Vayu), and Moksha (Jala). The four padas are like the four legs of a cow. Each Nakshatra represents a cow. The bull is represented by the Moon, who visits each Nakshatra from the first to the fourth pada, collectively representing Dharma.

During the Satya Yuga, all four legs of Dharma were strong. During the Dwapara Yuga, three were strong, during the Treta Yuga, two were strong, and now, during the Kali Yuga, only one leg of Dharma is strong. So, during the Kali Yuga, it is not just enough to see the

Janma Nakshatra but also the pada in which the native was born because only one pada is strong. The rest of the padas are weak.

Here is an example to explain how padas affect natives born in the same Nakshatra. Suppose a person's Janma Nakshatra is Ashwini, first pada. Now, this pada is the Agni pada, which stands for Dharma. So, for this person, Dharma will have a high focus in their life because the other padas, namely Artha, Kama, and Moksha, will be weak.

Similarly, suppose the native was born in the second pada of Ashwini Nakshatra. Then, Artha will be strong for them, and the other three will be weak. Again, if the native is born in Ashwini Nakshatra, the third pada, the Kama aspect will be strong because the others will be weak. For a person born in the fourth pada, Moksha's focus will be strong, and the other three will be weak. That is why it is important to focus on the pada and the Nakshatra to arrive at an accurate birth chart.

The First Nine Nakshatras – Janma Nakshatras

The 27 Nakshatras are divided into nine sets of three Nakshatras each. Everyone has a Janma Nakshatra or the Birth Star. It is the constellation in which the Moon was passing through at the time of one's birth. Janma Nakshatra is the primary driver of personal perceptions, behaviors, prejudices, and instincts and significantly impacts lives.

Janma Nakshatra governs the realities and experiences of life and the way one's mind works. Every constellation has a unique personality composed of likes, dislikes, skill sets, and more. Each Nakshatra has its strengths and weaknesses. None are perfect.

Every Janma Nakshatra has two corresponding constellations linked to it, referred to as Anujanma Nakshatra and Trijanma Nakshatra. For example, if you are born in the first Nakshatra, namely Ashwini, this becomes your Janma Nakshatra. Your Anujanma

Nakshatra will be the tenth constellation from Ashwini, namely Makam, and your Trijanma Nakshatra will be the nineteenth constellation, Moolam.

In the same way, each of the 27 Nakshatras has Anujanma and Trijanma Nakshatras linked to it. Here is a list of the first nine constellations. The first column is the Janma Nakshatra, the second column is the Anujanma Nakshatra, and the third column is the Trijanma Nakshatra.

Ashwini – Makam – Moolam

Bharani – Purva Phalguni – Purvashada

Krittika – Uttara Phalguni – Uttarashada

Rohini – Hastha – Shravana

Mrigashirsha – Chitra – Dhanishta

Ardra – Swathi – Satabhishtha

Punarvasu – Vishakha – Purva Bhadrapada

Pushya – Anuradha – Uttara Bhadrapada

Ashlesha – Jyeshtha – Revati

So, the first nine Nakshatras' Anujanma and Trijanma are listed here. Now, suppose your Janma Nakshatra is in the second column of the second set of nine Nakshatras. Then, your Anujanma and Trijanma Nakshatras will be the ones listed in the third and first columns, respectively.

For example, if your Janma Nakshatra is Hashtha, your Anujanma Nakshatra will be Shravana, and your Trijanma Nakshatra will be Rohini. Similarly, if your Janma Nakshatra is Purvashada, your Anujanma and Trijanma Nakshatras will be Bharani and Purva Phalguni, respectively. This chapter deals with the first Nakshatras or the first planetary group.

Every Nakshatra has a symbol assigned to it by the ancient rishis. Each of the symbols and glyphs refers to a particular aspect of human experience connected to the Nakshatra. Multiple symbols are often associated with each Nakshatra considering they affect many areas of human life and experience.

The animal symbol denoted to Nakshatras has a deep meaning to the asterism's nature and character, including its behavioral pattern. The animal connected with each Nakshatra gives a striking indication of the asterism's personality, behavior, and relationships with other constellations.

The Nakshatras are also divided into male and female energies. The masculine Nakshatras are more dynamic than the feminine Nakshatras, which are more passive.

Ashwini

Ashwini occupies 0 degrees to 13 degrees, 20 seconds in Mesha Rashi. The traditional symbol of Ashwini is the head of a horse. It represents the head and is symbolic of the start of the Zodiac. The glyph representing the symbol of Ashwini Nakshatra also stands for the female reproductive system relating to the beginning and initiation of all things.

The activities or actions suitable to be done in Ashwini Nakshatra are:

- Installing an idol or deity or "avahani"
- Thread ceremony or upanayanam
- Parting of the hair on the head or "simontan"
- Shaving or "cuda karanam"
- Starting education or "vidyarambham"

Ashwini is a godly masculine star and has an auspicious nature. Its animal symbol is a horse. The Ashwini Kumaras—to which this star is related—ride a golden chariot, bringing light, happiness, and healing to people. This star denotes the light of dawn, miracle performances, and transportation of goods. The direction of this asterism is forward.

Under the influence of Ashwini Nakshatra, people tend to be full of energy and are ready for adventure and taking risks. It is difficult for them to remain still as they get restless and impatient. They can behave immaturely and do irresponsible acts. This star controls all forms of transportation.

Bharani

Ranging from 13 degrees, 20 seconds to 26 degrees, 40 seconds in Mesha Rashi, Bharani Nakshatra stands for birth, death, and transformation represented by the yoni symbol encapsulated in a triangle. Yoni represents the female vagina, womb, or abode and stands for the feminine reproductive power. The triangle represents the three stars collectively known as the "Buckle of Isis" that make up this constellation or asterism. Ancient astrologers perceived this star as a portal between worlds.

Bharani, a feminine asterism, is good for doing the following activities:

- Nefarious and violent acts
- Entering a tunnel or cave
- Reconcilement activities
- Indulging in swindling and murdering people
- Distilling poison and poisonous medicines
- Activities related to weapons and fire

The direction of this asterism is downward-looking. It has a dreadful nature, and its symbol of a womb represents its ability to hide or eclipse things. The ideas associated with Bharani Nakshatra are suffering and struggle. Ruled by the Lord of Death, Yama, a native of this Nakshatra are usually entangled in the materialistic world. Its animal symbol is an elephant. It is considered the "star of restraint."

Under the influence of Bharani, people tend to struggle through the process of personal growth and transformation. They tend to have self-doubt and be jealous of others, but they are honest and disciplined natives and generally tend to give much importance to their opinions and ideas.

Krittika

Ranging from 26 degrees, 40 seconds in Mesha Rashi to 10 degrees in Vrishabha Rashi, Krittika Nakshatra is represented by a blade or flame metaphorically meaning the "one who cuts." The symbol of Krittika Nakshatra represents its proactive, fiery, and sharp nature.

Krittika's nature is violent, and its direction is downward-looking. This female constellation has a soft/harsh mix of temperament. Krittika means "ax" and represents the physical and creative forces needed to achieve great accomplishments. Ruled by the god of fire, Agni, Krittika asterism brings a burning sensation to the body and mind. This asterism, which has a sheep for its animal symbol, is suitable for the following activities/actions:

- Nefarious and violent activities
- Separation-related and reconciliations activities
- Battles

Considered to be the "star of fire," under the influence of Krittika, people are usually ambitious, passionate, and work determinedly toward their goals. They make great protectors and tend to take very good care of the people they love and are close to.

Rohini

Ranging from 10 degrees to 23 degrees, 20 seconds in Vrishabha Rashi, Rohini is the most materialistic constellation in the Zodiac. Its symbol is the chariot or ox-cart, and the glyph representing Rohini Nakshatra is a four-petaled flower. This glyph is connected to the number four and a rose, the typical emblem of Rohini. Rohini Nakshatra represents the Taurean features of stability, abundance, and fertility. Rohini's animal symbol is a serpent.

Rohini is a female Nakshatra and is suitable for the following activities:

- Installation of a deity/idol
- Thread ceremonies
- House constructions
- Marriages
- Coronations
- Activities of a permanent nature

It has a fixed nature, and natives born in Rohini are likely to be strong and responsible. Its direction is upward-looking and is ruled by Lord Brahma, the creator and the universe's engineer. Rohini is considered to be the "star of ascent." People under Rohini's influence are charming, beautiful, creative, talented, and follow a high standard of living. They are also generally critical of people and look down on others.

Mrigashirsha

Mrigashirsha Nakshatra ranges from 23 degrees, 20 seconds in Vrishabha Rashi up to 6 degrees, 40 seconds in Mithuna Rashi, the symbol of Mrigashirsha is a deer's head. Its glyph resembles a wine cup with a curved surface. The curved surface stands for the deer motif and the horns of Taurus, the bull. Activities suitable for Mrigashirsha are:

- Installation of idol/deity
- Thread ceremonies, marriages
- Travel
- Working with elephants and camels

Its direction is forward-looking. "Mrga" in the name translates to "deer," which means natives usually have an attractive face. This asterism has a soft nature, and natives are typically gentle and involved with research, the poetic, and artworks. This feminine Nakshatra has a serpent as its animal symbol.

Under the influence of Mrigashirsha, people love to travel, seeking new knowledge, and trying to understand their life. They continuously collect and increase their possessions. They are intelligent and are known to uncover hidden things easily.

Ardra

Ranging from 6 degrees, 20 seconds to 20 degrees in Mithuna Rashi, the symbol of Ardra Nakshatra is a teardrop. The teardrop or raindrop glyph has a diamond within it, representing this constellation's theme of growth and renewal through turbulence and chaos.

Ardra, another female Nakshatra, is good for activities like reconcilements and separations and surgical operations. It has a harsh and detestable nature. Its direction is upward-looking and is ruled by Lord Shiva, the destroyer. The animal symbol of Ardra is a dog.

The teardrop symbol of Ardra can also be taken to mean that this asterism is related to the pain and tears of others either by causing them pain or by feeling or empathizing the pain of others; however, the former is more prevalent among natives. Ardra rules over thieves, murderers, and those who create disorder.

Under the influence of Ardra Nakshatra, people are usually quite destructive, but they grow and develop through destruction and suffering. They are also great at using misfortune and difficult situations to their benefit. They are quite distant emotionally and come across as cold and stern.

Punarvasu

Punarvasu Nakshatra ranges from 20 degrees in Mithuna Rashi up to 3 degrees, 20 seconds in Karkataka Rashi. Its symbol is a quiver representing the holder of magical weapons that return to its original abode after completing their mission. The glyph of Punarvasu represents a circular path that shows an arrow leaving the quiver and returning to it, thereby completing the circle. The theme of Punarvasu is that of "becoming good again." Its glyph represents using, recovering, and recycling.

Punarvasu is a godly star and is good for the following activities:
- Thread ceremonies and marriages
- House constructions
- Changing places like moving into new homes, offices, or cities

Its direction is forward-looking and is ruled by Aditi, the mother of the devas. "Puna" translates to "repeat." Hence, Punarvasu is referred to as the "star of renewal." Natives born under Punarvasu usually change homes or professions or even personalities and do not like to be tied down. The star also stands for purification of self. This male Nakshatra's animal symbol is a cat.

Under the influence of Punarvasu, people are typically adept at overcoming challenging and difficult situations. They are inspirational, kind, and have a positive perspective on life. They are quite popular and have a forgiving nature. Also, they are usually content with their lot.

Pushya

Located between 3 degrees, 20 seconds, and 16 degrees, 40 seconds in Karkata Rashi, the symbol of Pushya is a cow's udder. The glyph of Pushya is a circle held within an open four-petaled flower—standing for the four tits of a cow's udder. The circle can be seen as a coconut, a drop of milk, or a wheel, all of which align with Pushya's theme of kindness, generosity, and nourishment.

Pushya is an auspicious star suitable for multiple auspicious beginnings like entering a new home (gruhapravesam), marriages, installation of a deity or idol, etc. When Pushya Nakshatra falls on a Thursday, it is considered an excellent time for all auspicious activities. It is a gentle asterism ruled over by Brihaspati, the guru of the devas. Its direction is upward-looking.

This asterism is believed to be the best among the 27 stars and stands for productivity and nourishment. Natives born in Pushya Nakshatra usually live a happy, flourishing life and can provide for others. Pushya is a masculine Nakshatra, and its animal symbol is a sheep.

Under the influence of Pushya Nakshatra, people give great importance to religion and their beliefs. They are quite arrogant with disagreeing opinions and tend to think they are always right, but they are kind and helpful toward people in need.

Ashlesha

Ashlesha Nakshatra is located between 16 degrees, 40 seconds to 30 degrees in Karkata Rashi. Its symbol is a serpent, which stands for coiling or embracing. Its glyph is represented by two symmetrically intercoiling lines, like the shape of the double-helix DNA. Ashlesha Nakshatra stands for transformative potential and intuition. Ashlesha Nakshatra is feminine, and its animal symbol is a cat.

The activities associated with Ashlesha are argumentation, gambling, falsehood, trade and commerce, burning, and anger. Its direction is downward-looking, and this asterism has a harsh nature. Ashlesha is a demonic star symbolized by a serpent. Natives born in Ashlesha can be anti-social but choose to live an austere life. Ashlesha can bring about pain but also has the potential for great transcendental aspirations.

Ashlesha is considered the "clinging star." People are usually intelligent and wise under its influence, but they often use their knowledge of dark deeds. They also tend to lie and be cunning. However, in the end, they pay for their misdeeds, and through these pains, they grow and develop. They hate being humiliated or criticized.

Chapter 4: Anujanma Nakshatras: The Second Nakshatra Group

The Second Nakshatra Group includes Magha, Purva Pahlguni, Uttara Phalguni, Hasta, Chitra, Swati, Vishakha, Anuradha, and Jyeshtha.

Magha

Magha Nakshatra ranges from 0 degrees to 13 degrees, 20 seconds in Simha Rashi. Its symbol is a throne, and its glyph is a three-pointed crown representing Leonine traits of kingship, honor, pride, duty, respect, and a high position in any hierarchy. Magha is a feminine asterism, and its animal symbol is a rat. Magha is suitable for the following actions/activities:

- Collection works
- Agriculture
- Marriages
- Dances
- Battles

- Works and activities related to weapons and poisons

Its direction is downward-looking. Magha translates into the "mighty one." People born in this Nakshatra usually occupy high and important positions in society and their workplace. Magha stands for pride and dignity. He or she can carry forward family traditions and has the power to lord over the masses.

Natives born in Magha Nakshatra are typically very rich and live in luxury, surrounded by servants to do their bidding. They are learned and have high respect in society, but they fall prey to their attractions to the opposite sex, and their high self-opinion causes them to take on a deep-rooted hatred toward people.

Under Magha's influence, people usually like wealth and power and are willing to work hard to achieve them. They are driven by a need to be recognized wherever they go. They are very loyal to the people they care for.

Purva Pahlguni

Ranging from 13 degrees, 20 seconds to 26 degrees, 40 seconds in Simha Rashi, Purva Phalguni stands for pleasure, delight, comfort, and indulgence. Its symbol is a hammock, and its glyph is a three-curved hammock with a circle within the central upward-turning curve. This hammock or bed represents luxury and a period of relaxation after achieving worldly accomplishments.

This Nakshatra has feminine energy, and its animal symbol is a rat. Activities associated with Purva Phalguni Nakshatra are:

- Wars and battles
- Nefarious and violent activities
- Meat selling
- Swindling and cheating
- Works related to weapons and poisons

Ruled by Venus, the planet of beauty, natives of Purva Phalguni are usually attractive with an ability to sway and influence people sweetly. While the asterism has a nefarious and harsh nature, it is also a lucky star. Purva Phalguni translates to the "fruit of the tree." So, it has the power to bestow good fortune on people. Moreover, the asterism is ruled by Bhagya, the Demi-god of good luck.

Under the influence of Purva Phalguni, people are usually relaxed and carefree. They love to enjoy themselves. They are great communicators and love a hectic social life. They have long-lasting relationships, but they can be very lazy, even if they are talented and creative.

Uttara Phalguni

Uttara Phalguni ranges from 26 degrees, 40 seconds in Simha Rashi to 10 degrees in Kanya Rashi. Its symbol is a fig tree representing comfort and relaxation but with a sense of wisdom rather than indulgence as in Purva Phalguni. Uttara Phalguni is a female star, and its animal symbol is a bull.

The glyph of Uttara Phalguni looks like the three-curved hammock of Purva Phalguni, but the central curve is pointed upwards, and the circle is on top of it, representing an individual who has risen like the sun—unlike the circle in the previous Nakshatra that is blanketed in luxury. The activities associated with Uttara Phalguni are:

- Thread ceremonies
- Installation of idols and deities
- House constructions
- Marriages and coronations

Uttara Phalguni is often translated as a "fig tree" and stands for abundant good qualities and fruitful life. It is referred to as the "star of patronage" because it is focused on helping others. Under the influence of Uttara Phalguni, people are loving and good-natured. They love making friends and have great relationships—and thrive when they are in relationships. They hate being alone and are insecure when they are lonely.

Hasta

Hasta Nakshatra ranges from 10 degrees to 23 degrees, 20 seconds in Kanya Rashi. Its symbol is the human hand, representing work and activities performed by hands, including art and craft. Sometimes, Hasta's glyph is represented by a potter's wheel in the form of an empty circle and five-finger projections pointed upwards. The direction of Hasta is forward-looking.

Hasta is a female asterism, and its animal symbol is buffalo. This asterism is good for the following activities:

- Thread ceremonies
- Construction of houses
- Deity/idol installation
- Marriages
- Coronations

Hasta's hand symbol is often represented as a clenched fist that translates to purity in thought and the power to control. It is deva or godly asterism and has a pleasant temperament. Hasta natives are skilled with their hands, likable and popular, and can remove ignorance and heal.

They are quite orthodox and conservative in their outlook and are inclined toward artistry and public service. They are eloquent speakers and fond of foreign countries. Under the influence of Hasta Nakshatra, people tend to be intelligent and talented. They learn things quickly. They find it difficult to let go of feelings and things. They like to be in professions where they can help others.

Chitra

Chitra Nakshatra ranges from 23 degrees, 20 seconds in Kanya Rashi to 6 degrees, 40 seconds in Tula Rashi. Its symbol is a jewel and is represented by a jewel star. It represents the mind of an artist who is continuously imagining and creating new designs, forms, illusions, and ideas. This feminine constellation is good for the following activities:

- Thread ceremonies
- House constructions
- Installation of idols and deities
- Entering a new home or gruhapravesam

Chitra translates to "beautiful" or "brilliant." It confers a beautiful picture and the ability to arrange things aesthetically. Vishwakarma, the cosmic architect, rules the soft-natured Chitra. Its animal symbol is a tigress.

Under the influence of Chitra, people are typically beautiful and charming. They express themselves well and are good communicators. With a good imagination, natives of Chitra are usually quite artistic. They are excellent at creating new things. The direction of Chitra is forward-looking.

Swati

Swati ranges from 6 degrees, 40 seconds to 20 degrees in Tula Rashi. Its symbol is a coral, and its glyph—a curved line intersecting with a straight line—represents a young shoot being blown by the wind or struck by a sword. The intersection of the curved and straight lines also stands for the balance of contrasting elements and forces. Swati is located halfway through the Nakshatra cycle and connected to compromises and crossroads. The direction of Swati is downward-looking.

Swati, a godly feminine star, is auspicious for the following activities:

- Thread ceremonies
- Entering a new home or gruhapravesam
- House constructions
- Installation of idols and deities
- Marriages

Swati translates to "sword" or "priest." Natives of Swati can cut themselves off from materialism. They love to travel and are learned. Swati natives are self-motivated and have independence in both thought and action. Ruled by Vayu, the wind god, Swat natives are usually slow and deliberate in their movements. The animal symbol of this asterism is the buffalo.

People under the influence of Swati make great artists and are good communicators. They are always curious, which paves the way for them to become learned and scholarly. While they are intuitive and have sharp instincts, Swati natives can also be egoistic and shallow.

Vishakha

Ranging from 20 degrees in Tula Rashi to 3 degrees, 20 seconds in Vrishchika Rashi, Vishakha's symbol is an arch. Its glyph is represented by a triumphal arch, which translates to "two-branched." The Nakshatra itself relates to the single-minded focus needed to achieve goals and the required painful sacrifices for the same. This feminine star has the animal symbol of a tiger. Vishakha is good for the following activities:

- Singing and dancing
- Writing
- Collecting commercial items
- Mechanical works

The direction of Vishakha is downward-looking. Considered the "star of purpose," Vishakha natives are driven by their goals and ambitions. They work hard to achieve their goals. They enjoy competitions and do not back down easily, but they get jealous of others and angry if things don't work out their way.

Vishakha natives are successful even if they are a bit self-centered. A tree with wide-spreading branches often symbolizes Vishakha. This symbol suggests that people under the influence of Vishakha grow in influence and will not stop until their efforts bear fruit.

Anuradha

Anuradha ranges from 3 degrees, 20 seconds to 16 degrees, 40 seconds in Vrischika Rashi. Its symbol is a lotus, and its glyph is also represented by a stick or staff with two young leaves protruding on either side of it. Anuradha reflects "success achieved subsequent" to the single-minded focus of Vishakha. Anuradha is a male Nakshatra, and its animal symbol is a rabbit. Sometimes, the animal symbol of Anuradha is taken to be a female deer. This asterism is good for the following activities:

- Marriages
- Gruhapravesam
- Thread ceremonies
- Reconcilements and separations
- House construction
- Installation of idols and deities

Its direction is forward-looking and is ruled by Mitra, a demigod associated with the sun god. Anuradha is considered to be the "star of calling others to action" and the "star of success." People born in Anuradha Nakshatra are great at organizing, and hence, make excellent leaders. Radha is the feminine energy that encourages everyone to serve the lord.

Under the influence of Anuradha, people are generally great organizers. They balance their work and relationships very well. They are flexible and can cooperate with others easily, both useful elements in teamwork, which, in turn, make them great leaders. They love to make friends and are good at sharing.

The stick or staff also stands for a magician's wand. Anuradha has the power to convert Vishakha's narrow-minded goal-oriented approach to a wide vision of awe and reverence for the entire universe.

Jyeshtha

Ranging from 16 degrees, 40 seconds to 30 degrees in Vrischika Rashi, Jyeshtha translates to "the eldest" and stands for authority. Its symbol is an amulet, and its glyph is a double-edged circular earring-like amulet with three lines connecting the outer and inner circles. Jyeshtha Nakshatra represents experience, expertise, and seniority. The three lines stand for the past, present, and future.

Jyeshtha is a female asterism, and its animal symbol is the rabbit. Often, its animal symbol is also taken to be a male deer. Jyeshtha is an auspicious star for the following activities:

- Commerce
- Writing
- Mechanical works
- Dancing and music

Jyeshtha Nakshatra has a sharp and forceful nature. Translating to "chief" or "senior-most," Jyeshtha Nakshatra confers natives with the power to achieve executive positions in their professions. Jyeshtha natives invariably get what they want. The star is ruled by Lord Indra, who bestows the power to get things done with goals achieved skillfully.

Under the influence of Jyeshtha Nakshatra, people tend to be great at wielding power and responsibility positions. Wise and intelligent, they are skilled at looking after their families and the people they care for. They are typically leaders of their house and their professional teams, but they tend to face many difficulties and hardships in their lives. They are not very social beings and have only a handful of trusted people around them.

Influence of Anujanma Nakshatras

The Anujanma Nakshatras stands for intervening elements that connect the past karma of a native and their present karma. The Anujanma Nakshatra demonstrates the potency or ability of a native to analyze, execute, and achieve the present's karma as connected with the past. The planets of the Anujamna Nakshatra should not be inimical with the planets of the Janma Nakshatra.

For example, if a native has Saturn in their Lagna or the house of the planet of their birth star, and Mars is in the fourth-star house from their Lagna, the chances of such individuals to make rash and wrong decisions are high. This happens because Mars and Saturn are inimical, with one in the Janma Nakshatra and the other in the Anujanma Nakshatra.

Chapter 5: Trijanma Nakshatras: The Last Nakshatra Group

The last group of Nakshatras forming the Trijanma Nakshatras for the first group include Moola, Purvashada, Uttarashada, Shravana, Dhanishta, Shatabishtha, Purva Bhadrapada, Uttara Bhadrapada, and Revati.

Moola

Located in the Dhanush Rashi (Sagittarius) from 0 degrees to 13 degrees, 20 seconds, Moola Nakshatra stands for "root" or "center" and is often referred to as the "root star." This Nakshatra represents the galactic center. Rightly so, the symbol of Moola is a bundle of roots.

The symbol is represented by three straight lines passing through the circumference and intersecting at the center of a circle. Two of the three straight lines bend and form lines that appear to meet toward each other. This glyph of a bundle of roots stands for Moola's desire to seek and discover the essential nature of all things in the universe. Additionally, roots also represent medicine. Moola, a masculine star, is good for the following activities:

- Acts of violence and nefariousness
- War
- Marriages
- Medication

Its direction is downward-looking, and its animal symbol is a dog. Under the influence of Moola, people seek the core principle of all things in life. The bundle of roots also stands for the natives' feelings of being tied or bound to misfortunes and suffering. Moola's nature is sharp and violent. Natives of Moola Nakshatra are clever, capable, and even spiritually devoted, but they always look at everything around them with a sense of mistrust.

Moola influences people to be good investigators who are skilled at uncovering hidden truths. The various ups and downs they face make them feel a deep sense of loss and pain. They are usually resentful and often blame others for their problems.

Purvashada

Purvashada Nakshatra extends from 13 degrees, 20 seconds to 26 degrees, 40 seconds in Dhanush Rashi. Its symbol is a fan, and its glyph is represented by a figure of eight, with the top circle being larger than the bottom circle. Another circle is embedded in the top curvature of the number eight. This glyph looks like a seashell from which Venus, the ruling planet of this Nakshatra, emerges. It also resembles the symbol of Purvashada, namely a fan.

Referred to as the "invincible star" and represented by a monkey, Purvashada is good for the following activities:

- Work concerning weapons and poisons
- Murder and killing actions
- Swindling and cheating

Its direction is downward-looking, and it has a violent, argumentative nature. Natives are typically humble and have a large family. They are faithful in their relationships and are likely to sit in high positions at their workplace and in society.

Under the influence of Purvashada, people are strong and independent. They continually strive hard to improve their status. With great communication, natives have good manipulation and influencing skills, but they tend to have anger issues and get aggressive.

The fan symbol of Purvashada has multiple connotations. It could be used to stoke the fire to keep the passion alive or to cool off the fire, which means to survive adversity, as a decorative item (standing for art and crafts), or as a symbol of mystery by hiding one's face behind the fan.

Uttarashada

Ranging from 26 degrees, 20 seconds in Dhanush Rashi up to 10 degrees in Makar Rashi (Capricorn), Uttarashada's symbol is a tusk. Its glyph is represented by two elephant tusks crossing over each other on a pyramid, rising from between the tusks. The pyramid represents the crystallization of power, the tusks stand for Lord Ganesha, the remover of obstacles, and the sun is the ruling planet of Uttarashada.

Uttarashada is a masculine star with a mongoose as its animal symbol. Its direction is upward-looking, and it has an auspicious nature. Ruled by the Sun God, Uttarashada reflects leadership qualities. It is referred to as the "universal star," which means natives can relate to others and work toward uplifting people around them. Uttarashada is good for:

- Deity/idol installation
- Marriages and coronations

Under the influence of Uttarashada, people are typically kind, soft-natured, and patient. They have immense enduring power. They are responsible and work hard with a determination to achieve their goals.

They are truthful and sincere, but if they lose interest in what they are doing, they become lazy.

Shravana

The meaning of Shravana is "to listen," and its symbol is an ear. This Nakshatra ranges from 10 degrees to 23 degrees, 20 seconds in Makar Rashi, and it stands for not only listening to others but also listening to one's inner voice.

Its glyph is represented by the full moon, its ruling planet, supported underneath by a crescent moon. Three uneven straight lines emerge from the circumference of the full moon. The three straight lines have a small circle at their ends. The small circles represent the "three uneven steps" connected to Shravana. The three lines represent the connection between the speaker and the listener.

Shravana is a masculine star, and its animal symbol is a monkey. Shravana is believed to be the "star of learning" and has a deep connection to Goddess Saraswati and Lord Vishnu in his dwarf form. Shravana stands for understanding and communication of that knowledge, which helps people to transcend the material world.

Under its influence, people are usually wise and intelligent. They always seek knowledge, are good listeners, and make good teachers. They are usually quite restless and want to travel from place to place in search of new knowledge.

Dhanishta

Dhanishta ranges from 23 degrees, 20 seconds in Makar Rashi up to 6 degrees, 40 seconds in Kumbh Rashi (Aquarius). Its symbol is a drum, and its glyph also represents a drum. From the side, the glyph of Dhanishta looks like a standing drum with three intersecting lines. Dhanishta is a bold and confident Nakshatra and stands for music and dance, representing the larger rhythm of life.

The glyph also represents the rhomboid pattern of the placement of the stars in this constellation. The three intersecting lines on the transverse angle of the standing drum form eight unequal triangles.

These triangles represent the eight Vasus, the presiding deities of Dhanishta.

Dhanishta is a female constellation with a lion as its animal symbol. It is a good star for the following activities:

- Upanayanam or thread ceremonies
- Gruha pravesam or entering a new home
- Taking medication
- House construction

Its direction is upward-looking, and the planet Mars rules it. The symbol of a drum represents talent or an interest in music and dance. It is referred to as the "star of the symphony," which also stands for the natives' ability to unify people toward a common cause.

Under the influence of Dhanishta, people are wealthy and have many possessions. They are artistic and inclined to music and dance, but like the drum—its symbol—natives tend to be hollow and are continually looking for external things to fill this emptiness, an attitude that makes them highly self-absorbed.

Shatabhisha

Ranging from 6 degrees, 40 seconds to 20 degrees in Kumbha Rashi, Shatabhisha's symbol is 1,000 stars. Shatabhisha stands for a "hundred healers." Its glyph is an empty circle from which four lightning bolts emerge, representing the presence of electricity in everything. Two small circles adorn the top and bottom of the circular glyph. These little circles represent electrons going around the atomic nucleus.

From above, the glyph of Shatabhisha looks like a turtle with its four limbs outstretched. The turtle is seen as a carrier of the world. The glyph stands for the transpersonal nature of this rather reclusive, eccentric, and mystical asterism.

Shatabisha is a female asterism, and its animal symbol is a mare. It is upward-looking and is good for the following activities:

- House construction
- Entering a new home
- Installing deities/idols
- Thread ceremonies
- Taking medicines
- Horse riding

It has a cruel, detestable nature and is ruled by Rahu. Translating to "the hundred physicians," this Nakshatra represents physicians and healers. Referred to as the "veiling star," Shatabhisha reflects quietude and feelings of difficulties concerning self-expression.

Under the influence of Shatabhisha, people are generally philosophical and highly secretive. They can be great healers, but they are moody and lonely, considering they lack good communication skills. They also tend to have an unreasonably high opinion about themselves and believe they know everything, which comes across as arrogance.

Purva Bhadrapada

Purva Bhadrapada ranges from 20 degrees in Kumbha Rashi up to 3 degrees, 20 seconds in Meena Rashi (Pisces). Its symbol is a funeral cot or bed. Its glyph represents two faces of a man standing for the moment of death, during which one exists both in this world and in the next.

The glyph of a Purva Bhadrapada is a circle with a horizontal chord on the upper hemisphere, a vertical diagonal intersecting this chord, and two small, uneven horizontal lines intersecting the diagonal in the lower hemisphere. A sword also represents Purva Bhadrapada, and the diagonal of the circle represents the sword, which stands for severance.

Purva Bhadrapada is a masculine star with a lion as its animal symbol. It is a star for the following activities:

- Argument-related works
- Nefarious and violent tasks
- Meat selling
- Battles and wars
- Killing

It has a dreadful nature. The star translates to "the burning pair"—along with the next star, namely Uttara Bhadrapada—and represents an impetuous and passionate individual who usually has an unstable mind, but because Jupiter rules it, they tend to have a repentant nature and accept and learn from their mistakes. It is also referred to as the "star of transformation."

Under its influence, people are indulgent and passionate in all their works. They are quite secretive and two-faced. They are good communicators and can influence people.

Uttara Bhadrapada

Uttara Bhadrapada ranges from 3 degrees, 20 seconds to 16 degrees, 40 seconds in Meena Rashi. Its symbol is a water snake, and its glyph represents this. It is a serpentine, snake-like line slithering around and upward on a vertical axis, stick, or staff. The deity of this constellation is Ahirbudhanya, or the "Serpents of Death" represented in the glyph.

Like Purva Bhadrapada, Uttara Bhadrapada also connects to death, though in a different form. This asterism represents consciousness sinking deep into an abyss or the super consciousness. Uttara Bhadrapada stands for the deep levels of unconsciousness and the prana or life force within it.

This male asterism has a cow for its animal symbol and, together with Purva Bhadrapada, is referred to as the "burning pair." This star reflects the power to control anger and move from lower materialistic consciousness to higher spiritual consciousness.

Under its influence, people are generally good at controlling their emotions. They tend to be lazy but are cheerful and kind. They are highly protective of the people they love and care for. They love home and family and all the simple good things that come with their loved ones.

Revati

Revati Nakshatra ranges from 16 degrees, 40 seconds to 30 degrees in Meena Rashi. Its symbol is a fish, and its glyph is two intersecting circular sectors (fish-like) with an eye in the center. Revati also means "to transcend" and "wealth." Revati absorbs and synthesizes the mysteries of the previous 26 asterisms, an element represented by the all-seeing eye between the intersecting fish-like structures.

Revati is a female asterism and has an elephant for its animal symbol, which reflects material prosperity. Revati is related to the following activities:

- Thread ceremony
- Installation of idols/deities
- Recovering and overcoming drug addiction
- Gruha pravesam

Revati translates to "wealth" and is ruled by Pusha, a deva known for his shepherding and protecting nature. Under the influence of Revati, people are generally helpful, loving, and kind. They are positive people and have a happy disposition. They enjoy making new friends and love being social. They are caregivers too. Being the last Nakshatra, Revati indicates the final journey, from this world to the next.

Different Types of Karma

Karma is a supremely important element in Hinduism. A simple definition of karma is that it represents the fruits of one's past and present actions, which, in turn, impact the fruits of the future. The literal translation of "karma" is action in Sanskrit. There are typically three types of karma:

- Sanchita Karma
- Prarabdha Karma
- Aagami Karma

Sanchita Karma – This baggage of karma is accumulated past actions waiting to come to fruition. Sanchita is like a storehouse that holds all the actions of your past lifetimes. It is a collection of unresolved karmas waiting to achieve resolution status.

Prarabdha Karma – This karma is what you are doing now, in this lifetime, and the fruits of your present actions.

Agami Karma – Future actions resulting from your current karma are collectively referred to as Agami Karma. Resolving and mitigating past karma create new karmas that may or may not be resolved in this lifetime. The results of the current karmas carried into the future are referred to as Agami Karma.

The Janma Nakshatra, Anujanma Nakshatra, and the Trijanma Nakshatra are rooted in your past and present karmas. Of all the planets, Rahu and Ketu are considered the most closely associated with karmas and their fruitions. The ancient Vedic seers categorized these two shadow planets as the most mysterious heavenly bodies that profoundly affect people's lives, depending on their karmas, based on which they posit themselves on their birth chart.

Every one of the seven planets with a physical presence affects and influences your present life on Earth. On the other hand, Rahu and Ketu are believed to be "invisible" energy forms that can access karmas from past lives, namely the Sanchita Karmas.

Ketu is considered the oldest planet as he existed even at the time of cataclysms of nature. Therefore, all your past lives' karmas are recorded in Ketu's registry. His records indicate the area in which you have been working during previous lifetimes. Rahu, being the second oldest planet according to Vedic Astrology, holds the information regarding your future.

Therefore, Ketu gives an indication of talents, which you have been polishing up on in previous incarnations and come naturally in the present life. In summary, Ketu stores your past, and Rahu stores your future.

Effects of Planets in Various Houses

Here are some examples of how planets affect natives as they pass through the various houses of the Zodiac.

When Saturn is in the ninth house, he brings about losses in finance. Natives are likely to face obstacles when performing good actions. Close relatives could die, and there could be perpetual sorrow. In the tenth house, Saturn drives the natives to do some sinful action. Also, there could be a loss of honor for natives. They could suffer from diseases.

Saturn in the eleventh house brings happiness and wealth to the natives. They are likely to receive great honors too. Saturn in the twelfth house is likely to drive the natives to pursue worthless and fruitless businesses. Natives are likely to be robbed of their wealth, and spouses and children could fall sick.

Rahu in the Janma Rashi or the first house brings about death or sickness. In the second, fifth, seventh, and ninth houses, natives lose wealth, money, etc. In the third, sixth, and eleventh houses, Rahu brings happiness. In the fourth, he brings sorrow. Rahu in the eighth house brings danger to the life of the native. In the tenth house, Rahu brings about gain for the natives. In the twelfth house, Rahu brings about expenditure.

Sun and Mars affect the natives only during the first 10 degrees of a house, whereas Venus and Jupiter affect when they are in the center of the house, and the powers of Saturn and Moon are effective when they are in the last part—last 10 degrees of the Zodiac—through which they are passing. The effect of Rahu and Mercury are felt right across the 30 degrees of any given Zodiac.

PART THREE: Lunar Mansions in Predictive Astrology

Chapter 6: Timing of Events: Udu-Dashas

Predictive Astrology or Phalita Jyotishya—which translates to "that which will fructify"—deals with karma, actions, and behaviors that define one's destiny. This sub-branch of astrology also deals with how you can reverse earlier mistakes and wrongdoings through penance, worship, charity, etc.

Your horoscope is like a snapshot of the heavens, as seen from your place and time of birth. However, the planets are not fixed or frozen. They are continuously moving. Hindu Astrology, therefore, has two types of movements of Grahas or planets. One type is called transits or direct movement of planets in its ecliptic. Another type of movement is referred to as progressed or projected movement, which, in Vedic Astrology, is termed as Dashas.

Timing of Events is a unique feature of Vedic Astrology. Vimshottari Dasha is an essential tool and technique used in Jyotishya to time events. This highly popular system has been in use for centuries and is employed both by amateurs, in its basic forms, and professional astrologers, in its advanced and basic forms.

Vimshottari Dasha is based on the Moon or Chandra's position on a Nakshatra, and therefore, is a Nakshatra Dasha. The first Nakshatra—as you already know—is Ashwini, which is ruled by Ketu. The second Nakshatra is Bharani, ruled by Venus or Shukra. This list continues until the 27th Nakshatra, Revati, ruled by Mercury or Bhuddh. Another popular Dasha is called Kalachakra, and it incorporates both Rashis and Nakshatras.

Understanding Udu Dasha

Udu translates to "flying," a term also used for Nakshatras. Ideally, all Nakshatra Dashas are Udu Dasha. However, in practice, Vimshottari Dasha is considered to the "The Udu Dasha." Astrologers have used this Dasha as the primary staple for centuries. However, in recent times, astrologers like B V Raman, Sri Sanjay Rath, and Sri K. N. Rao have studied and produced a large body of work dealing with multiple other Dashas.

The primary and most basic premise behind the concept of Dashas is this: Life is sectioned into different segments or periods represented by planets (Nakshatra Dasha) or signs (Rashi Dasha) in the horoscopes. The orientation point for Nakshatra Dasha is the natal moon. Now, visualize the moon's progress from the moment of a native's birth through the rest of the Zodiac at a slower speed than its direct movement speed, which is about two and a half days per sign.

As the Moon or Chandra passes through the different Nakshatras, the planet lordship also changes. The planetary lord or ruler is considered to be the main planet indicator during the period Chandra passes through that Nakshatra. Some Dashas, including the most popularly used, namely Vimshottari Dashas, have a very long total duration. For example, in the Vimshottari Dasha, the natal moon takes 120 years to transit through the entire Zodiac, and therefore, most individuals do not complete the entire cycle in their lifetime.

Vimshottari Dasha System and Nakshatras

According to the Vimshottari Dasha system, each of the nine planets in Vedic Astrology rule over varying periods, the total of which is 120 years.

- Ketu rulers for seven years
- Venus rules for twenty years
- The Sun rules for six years
- The Moon rules for ten years
- Mars rules for seven years
- Rahu rules for eighteen years
- Jupiter rules for sixteen years
- Saturn rules for nineteen years
- Mercury rules for seventeen years

Although there is no rationale behind the formation of the Vimshottari Dasha System and the ruling periods, some experts have grouped the periods into two categories by an imaginary line between the Moon and the orienting (or Udu) point in the Vimshottari scheme and have come up with the following:

- The periods of Saturn, Jupiter, Rahu, and Mars total 60 years – this is one category.

- The periods of the Moon, the Sun, Venus, Ketu, and Mercury total 60 years – this is the second category.

Therefore, the outer planets are placed in the first group while the two luminaries, namely the Sun and Moon, along with the inner planets, are placed in the second group. In the Udu Dasha system, the natal moon's sidereal constellation position is taken as the point at which the native enters the 120-year cycle. In the 360-degree ecliptic, there are 27 constellations measuring 13 degrees, 20 minutes each. It starts at Aries (0-degrees), which is ruled by Ketu.

Ketu is followed by Venus, Surya (Sun), Chandra (Moon), Mangala (Mars), Rahu, Jupiter (Guru), Shani (Saturn), and Mercury (Bhuddh) in the same order. This order repeats until all the 27 asterisms are covered. Each Vimshottari Dasha period (called mahadasha) is further subdivided into nine sub-periods called antardashas or bhuktis.

The first bhukti or antardasha is ruled by the lord of the mahadasha and is followed by the bhuktis of the remaining eight in the same order. For example, in the Sun's Mahadasha, the first antardasha will be ruled by Sun himself, followed by the Moon, Mars, Rahu, Jupiter, Saturn, Mercury, Venus, and Ketu.

Each of the antardashas can be further divided into antaras, pratyantaras, sukshmas, and more. However, going into these finer divisions' practical usefulness is far less than the cumbersomeness and uncertainty behind the accuracy of such data. Therefore, most astrologers do not go deeper than the antardasha period.

The Vimshottari Dasha System follows the power of the Lords who rule over the Nakshatras. Here is a list of the 27 Nakshatras and the planet lords that rule them for better understanding. This list is given planet-wise:

    1. Ketu rules over Ashwini, Magha, and the Moola (the first, tenth, and nineteenth Nakshatras)

    2. Venus or Shukra rules over Bharani, Purva Phalguni, and Purvashadam (the second, eleventh, and twentieth Nakshatras)

    3. Sun or Surya rules over Krittika, Uttara Phalguni, and Uttarashada (the third, twelfth, and 21st Nakshatras)

    4. Moon or Chandra rules over Rohini, Hasta, and Shravana (the fourth, thirteenth, and 22nd Nakshatras)

    5. Mars or Mangala is the lord of Mrigashirsa, Chitra, and Dhanista (the fifth, fourteenth, and 23rd Nakshatras)

6. Rahu is the lord of Ardra, Swati, and Shatabhishta (the sixth, fifteenth, and 24th Nakshatras)

7. Jupiter or Guru is the lord of Punarvasu, Vishakha, and Purva Bhadrapada (the seventh, sixteenth, and 25th Nakshatras)

8. Saturn of Shani is the lord of Pushya, Anuradha, and Uttara Bhadrapada (the eighth, seventeenth, and 26th Nakshatras)

9. Mercury or Bhuddh is the lord of Ashlesha, Jyestha, and Revati (the ninth, eighteenth, and 27th Nakshatras)

Therefore, Ketu, Venus, the Sun, the Moon, Mars, Rahu, Jupiter, Saturn, and Mercury—in that order—rule over three Nakshatras each. The three Nakshatras in one set, ruled by one planet lord, form the Janma, Anujanma, and Trijanma Nakshatras for each other. Further, every planet has a sign of exaltation Zodiac sign, which is as follows:

- The Sun's exaltation sign is Aries or Mesha Rashi
- The Moon's exaltation sign is Taurus or Vrishabha Rashi
- Rahu's exaltation sign is Gemini or Mithuna Rashi
- Jupiter's exaltation sign is Cancer or Karkata Rashi
- Mercury's exaltation sign is Virgo or Kanya Rashi
- Saturn's exaltation sign is Libra or Tula Rashi
- Ketu's exaltation sign is Sagittarius or Dhanush Rashi
- Mars's exaltation sign is Capricorn or Makar Rashi
- Shukra's exaltation sign is Pisces or Kumbha Rashi

Nakshatras and Planet Transits

The Navatara and Tara Bala system is a Nakshatra predictive system used to understand the planets' transits through the various Rashis. This system tracks the transits of important and key Nakshatras from the Lagna or the birth Nakshatra. For example, if your birth Nakshatra is Jyeshtha, this becomes your Janma Nakshatra, and the counting for the Navatara and Tara Bala system starts from Jyeshtha. Then, the first nine Nakshatras for you would be as follows:

1. Jyeshtha
2. Moola
3. Purvashada
4. Uttarashada
5. Shravana
6. Dhanishta
7. Shatabisha
8. Purva Bhadrapada
9. Uttara Bhadrapada

These first nine Nakshatra counted from your Janma Nakshatra hold far more potency to deliver effects than the second and third tier of nine Nakshatras. This concept, referred to as Udu-Dashas, has a deep connection to Dasas and planet transits.

Further, according to Andrew Foss, a Vedic Astrologer of high repute and author of the best-selling book *Yoga of the Planets*, these nine important aspects of your life are connected to planetary rulers and the sequence of the Dasha system. Read on to find out how the Dashas affect these nine important aspects of your life.

Janma or Your Birth – This crucial aspect of your life is related to the first house in the Udu-Dasha system. Mercury and Ketu influence this aspect. Your Janma is connected to your birth Nakshatra which, according to the Udu-Dasha system, becomes the first Nakshatra for you, and the tenth and the nineteenth asterisms, which are your Anujamna and Trijanma Nakshatras.

Your birth star governs everything in your life. Furthermore, the moon is connected to your mind, and the star under the moon's influence becomes the seat of your soul. The birth star and your first house represent a focused form of your ability to synthesize all your life experiences using your intelligence.

The ruler of this aspect, Mercury, also governs early childhood, and this planet's influence and position determine the status of your birth, the development of your thought process, and education during that time of your life.

Andrew Foss says this about the Janma Nakshatra: "It is the fruit empowered to fulfill our desires depending on what we deserve." Now, when Saturn transits through your birth star, it shakes up certain things in your life because Saturn is a natural enemy of Mercury and Ketu. Therefore, your health could be challenged, which can be seen as a reminder to seek liberation (or moksha) in this lifetime.

The birth star for most astrologers is a point of conflict. Some believe that the first house is beneficial, and some think it is malefic. Therefore, it makes sense to accept a balanced approach to this crucial house. The birth star mostly supports the native, yet the beneficial effects could fall prey to hidden challenges or connection to the eighth house.

Janma Nakshatras, which are one, ten, and nineteen, are connected to Mercury. If your birth Nakshatra is also ruled by Mercury, all the other asterisms owned by Mercury will have a Janma relationship in your horoscope.

Sampat - Sampat is related to gains. The status of your second and eleventh house—counted from Lagna—determines this factor in your life and is ruled by Venus. The Sampat houses are the second, eleventh, and twentieth Nakshatras from your Janma Nakshatra and are ruled by Venus. Number 2 in Vedic Astrology is always related to the accumulation of wealth, gains, and profits.

Therefore, in your Rashi Chart or birth chart, benefic planets placed here during their Dasas bring gains for you, and malefic planets could bring losses and a sense of deprivation. Transits through the second star are gainful for the native. Therefore, Jupiter transiting through the second star can be particularly profitable for the naïve as this planet is connected to good fortune, acquisitions, blessings, and prosperity.

To illustrate with an example, if your birth star is Swait, Jupiter will bring gains and profits when it is transiting through Vishakha. Similarly, for a native born in Jyestha Nakshatra, Moola would be the second Nakshatra, which means all Ketu stars will bring good fortune for this native whenever benefic planets transit through them.

Vipat - Another critical life element, Vipat, is all about dangers to your wealth and money. This aspect is connected to the eighth and twelfth houses, counted from your Lagna, and is ruled by Sun, the planet connected to wealth. Vipat Nakshatra is the third asterism from your natal moon. The third Nakshatra has the power to destroy adharma and people who do not follow dharma.

As it is ruled by the Sun, the planet related to wealth, the third Nakshatra position is important for obtaining or losing wealth. You already know that Sun and Saturn are bitter enemies. Therefore, it is easy to understand that you are likely to face significant financial problems when Saturn transits through the third house.

For example, if your Janma Nakshatra is Jyeshta, the third Nakshatra would be Purvashada. When Saturn transits through this Nakshatra, its energy to create financial problems for the concerned native will be triggered. Vimpat positions can lead to the native making bad decisions and putting forth multiple challenges for them during major transits like Saturn, Rahu, or Ketu. It is also connected to the twelfth house, which is also related to the loss of wealth. A positive way of looking at such seeming losses is that these difficult times drive one to look spiritually upwards and find their path to liberation.

Kshema - Kshema relates to happiness and security in your life, is connected to the fourth Nakshatra, and is ruled by Moon. The fourth, thirteenth, and 22nd Nakshatras from your birth star are related to Kshema, which is associated with a disease-free life of comfort and ease. The fourth Nakshatra is connected with the feelings of security that the native gets.

Therefore, when benefic planets like Jupiter and Venus transit through the fourth, thirteenth, and 22nd Nakshatras, the native may have a substantial improvement in their state of happiness. On the other hand, malefic planets like Ketu could result in unhappy disruptions to the native's life.

Prayatak - Prayatak is related to obstacles and enemies, is ruled by Mars, and is managed by the fifth, fourteenth, and 23rd Nakshatras from your Janma Nakshatra. This aspect of your life is connected to the third and sixth houses. It is related to enemies and rivals who can instill fear of destruction in the native.

Mars, the ruler of this position and aspect, is the lord who prevents you from violating your dharma. After all, no one really wants to do wrongful deeds to face the wrath of a weapon-wielding warrior like Mars. So, fear helps keep your adharma actions in check.

With Mars ruling this life aspect, there is bound to be frustrations and indecisions when Saturn, the enemy of Mars, transits through this Nakshatra. The primary objective of the fifth Nakshatra is to fight and compete to do your dharma. Therefore, if your birth Nakshatra is Vishakha when Saturn transits through Purvashada, you are likely to face the malefic effects of Saturn even if your Sade Sati is three signs away.

Sadhana - Sadhana is the fulfillment, accomplishments, and attainment of desires and is ruled by Rahu. The life element is connected to the eleventh house. Sadhana is managed by the sixth, fifteenth, and 24th Nakshatras from your birth asterism. Benefic planets transiting through the sixth Nakshatra will bring fruits, while malefic planets will bring forth struggle and prevent opportunities from being available.

Interestingly, because Rahu is connected to this Nakshatra, desires and accomplishments may be fulfilled through unethical and devious means. For example, if your birth star is Chitra, when Saturn transits through Purvashada—the sixth Nakshatra from your Janma Nakshatra—this period could get support through the transits, and your desires could lead to fruition, provided it all fits in with the context of your Dasha period.

Naidhana or Vadha - This interesting and important part of your life deals with changes driven by the death or destruction of old things and elements. It is ruled by Jupiter and is connected to the eighth house. It is represented by the seventh, sixteenth, and 23rd Nakshatras from your birth star.

When malefic planets like Rahu, Ketu, or Saturn transit through the seventh, sixteenth, and 23rd Nakshatras, the native is likely to face challenges. These life experiences are also connected to the eighth house from the Lagna, where malefic planets can bring about acute illnesses, sudden accidents, or divorces without warning. The eighth house experiences are excellent lessons for one to transcend beyond the mundane materialism and search for the true meaning and purpose of life.

Mitra - Life without partners and friends is not worth living. Your horoscope helps you determine how your friends and partners will help or harm you by studying the "mitra" aspect of your life, which Saturn rules and is related to the seventh house and the eighth, seventeenth, and 26th Nakshatras from your birth star.

Saturn appears to be an unusual ruler in this place, considering this aspect deals with friends and progress. Andrew Foss explains that the fulfillment of desire after waiting so long—in that you have forgotten you had the desire at all—is a reflection of Saturn's power to do good by making you work hard, responsibly, and with patience. His seemingly malign attitude shows that your laziness and irresponsible behavior will not bring your desires to fruition.

Param Mitra - This aspect deals with great friends and spiritual fulfillment. Ruled by Ketu, it is related to the ninth and twelfth houses from your Lagna and the ninth, eighteenth, and 27th Nakshatras from your Janma Nakshatra. In the ninth Nakshatra and ninth house, all planets support the native and bring good fortune.

The ninth Nakshatra is connected to Ketu, a planet reflecting the time and place where your karma's and desires' ultimate liberation and fruition are completed. The ninth house is the peak of your accomplishments. Benefic planets transiting through the ninth Nakshatra are bound to hold great promise for natives.

Importantly, Dasha's effects should be read or studied by themselves. You must refer to the birth chart and the transits. The stars of the dashas and the asterisms' and planet lords' dispositions represent sensitive areas in the concerned native's life. Therefore, all aspects of astrology have to be taken into account to arrive at accurate and sensible predictions.

Chapter 7: Nakshatras and Relationship Compatibility

Relationship and marriage compatibility is not just an interesting topic but an essential element in Predictive Vedic Astrology. In Indian culture, where arranged marriages are the norm, comparing horoscopes to see if the potential couple are suitable for each other is the starting point of any marriage plans. Moreover, multiple cases have proved the efficacy of horoscope comparisons before arranging marriages. The interest and the intrigue behind the concept are, of course, unmistakable. Therefore, this chapter is part of this book on Nakshatras.

Just to give you an overview at this juncture, there are 27 Nakshatras in the Zodiac, each having four padas or quarters. The asterisms are connected to different Rashis or Zodiac Signs, as well as the nine planets. The star in which you were born is referred to as the birth star. If you start counting from here, your birth star is #1. The tenth star from here counted in Nakshatras' accepted order—from Ashwini to Revati—will be your Anujanma Nakshatra, and the nineteenth asterism will be your Trijanma Nakshatra. These three asterisms are crucial components that are considered during the matchmaking of a bride and groom.

The nine asterisms starting from your birth star represent nine facets of human life, including Janma, Sampat, Vipat, Kshema, Pratyaka, Sadhana, Vata, Mitra, and Parama Mitra. Furthermore, the first nine nakshatras are referred to as the first pariraya, the second nine are called the second pariraya, and the third set of nine asterisms is called the third pariraya. This point plays an important during horoscope matching.

Two main types of relationships can be formed while matching horoscopes, namely Uttama (Best Relationships) and Madhyama (Moderate Relationships). The nakshatras of the boy and the girl are taken into consideration. The astrologer starts the count from the girl's Janma Nakshatra and counts until the boy's Janma Nakshatra.

If this count is four, six, or nine, which stands for Sadhana, Kshema, and Parama Mitra, the relationship is considered uttama or the best, and the marriage has a high chance of success. According to this counting structure, uttama relationships can be formed between the sixth, fifteenth, and 24th Nakshatras, the second, eleventh, and twentieth Nakshatras, and the ninth, eighteenth, and 27th Nakshatras.

If the count from the girl's to the boy's birth star is three, five, or seven, the relationship is believed to be bad, and the marriage proposal is rarely taken forward. More detailed layers need to be considered depending on which pariraya the Nakshatras of the girl and boy fall. In some cases, certain padas of the Nakshatras are considered good, while other padas are rejected.

The second type of relationship, called Madhyama or average, is formed when the boy's and girl's birth stars have a Janma, Anujanma, and Trijanma relationship with each other. Therefore, Madhyama relationships can be formed with the first, tenth, and nineteenth Nakshatras, the second, eleventh, and twentieth Nakshatras, and the eighth, seventeenth, and 26th Nakshatras.

An important rule is associated with the number 27, considering there are 27 Nakshatras in the Zodiac. If the count from the girl's Janma Nakshatra to the boy's is 27 and if Chandra is in the same sign for both, the marriage is likely to meet with success. However, if the Moon in the boy's Rashi Chart is in the twelfth house of the girl's Moon, the relationship will not be good.

If the girl and boy share the same Nakshatra, the following rules hold:

- **Uttama Relationships** – If the stars of both the girl and the boy are Rohini, Ardra, Magha, Hasta, Vishakha, Shravana, Uttara Bhadrapada, or Revati, the relationship will be the best or Uttama.

- **Madhyama Relationships** – If the stars of both the girl and boy are Ashwini, Krittika, Mrigashirsha, Pushya, Purvashada, or Uttarashada, the relationship will be moderate or Madhyama.

- **Atamam or Bad** – If both the girl and boy are of Bharani, Ashlesha, Swati, Jyeshta, Moola, Dhanishta, Shatabisha, or Purva Bhadrapada, the relationship is no good.

Ashtakoot Guna Milan

Ashtakoot Guna Milan is an astrological system used to match the compatibility factors between prospective brides and grooms. This method uses the Moon Chart, the Moon Sign, or Rashi and the prospective couple's birth stars to assess the compatibility between them. There are eight factors called Koots, consisting of 36 Gunas, that are taken into account while calculating the Guna, namely:

1. **Varna Koot** – This element is related to ego and reflects the individual's personality and background.

2. **Vashya Koot** – Vashya Koot is about power and relates to the power equation and controlling person between the couple.

3. **Tara Koot** – This element reflects the friendship between the Nakshatras of the bride and groom. It talks about the proximity between the two stars.

4. Yoni Koot – This element is all about the sexual attraction between the prospective bride and groom.

5. Graha-Maitri Koot – This is related to the harmony between the Rashi charts of the girl and boy.

6. Gana Koot – This element is connected to the temperament and behavior of the boy and girl.

7. Bhakoot – This element is about love and is connected to the boy's and girl's Rashi Moon positions.

8. Nadi Koot – This is connected to the health and genes of the prospective couple.

The weightage given to each of these factors is the same as the serial number against them, and the maximum score is 36.

The Asktakoot Guna Milan calculates the Guna and arrives at a score for the match, which can be an indicator of the marriage's future. If the score is less than eighteen, the marriage is not likely to be successful. A score between eighteen and 24 reflects an average marriage.

A score of about 24 suggests that the marriage has a high potential for success, with the couple being happy in their relationship. Scores between 25-32 are good, while those between 32 and 36 are considered exceptional, and the marriage is destined for success. Now, look at the eight Koots in more detail.

Varna Koot – The Varna is a determining factor of an individual's ego and personality according to their Zodiac sign. According to Vedic Astrology, Zodiac signs are divided into four Varnas, namely Brahmin, Kshatriya, Vaishya, and Shudra, in descending order of hierarchy.

- Cancer (Karkata Rashi), Scorpio (Vrischika Rashi), and Pisces (Meena Rashi) belong to the Brahmin Varna
- Aries (Mesha Rashi), Leo (Simha Rashi), and Sagittarius (Dhanush Rashi) belong to the Kshatriya Varna

- Taurus (Vrishabha Rashi), Virgo (Kanya Rashi), and Capricorn (Makar Rashi) belong to the Vaishya Varna.

- Gemini (Mithuna Rashi), Aquarius (Kumbh Rashi), and Libra (Tula Rashi) belong to the Shudra Varna

Marriages made between a girl and a boy within the same Varna are considered to be auspicious. If the groom's Varna is higher than the bride's, the match is considered approachable. However, if the bride's Varna is higher than the boy's, it signifies an inauspicious marriage.

Vashya Koot - This category of Guna compatibility is a reflection of who will dominate in the marriage. It is not just domination over a partner but the power of holding the reins attractively and sensibly to make a success of the marriage. Holding 2 points, this category involves Zodiac signs and their connection to five types of animals, including the following:

- Chatushpada (translates to four-footed) - Aries, Taurus, the first half of Capricorn, and Sagittarius's second half

- Human - Gemini, Virgo, Libra, Aquarius, and the first half of Sagittarius

- Jalchar (water animals) - Cancer, Pisces, and the second half of Capricorn

- Vanacara (jungle or wild animals) - Leo

- Keet (worms) - Scorpio

There is a scoring system when the Zodiac signs of the bride and groom are matched. For example, if the bride and groom both have Zodiac signs in the Chatuspada category, the score is 2—which is the maximum allocated for this Koot. There are 25 such combinations, and each combination is given a score ranging from 0 to 2.

Simply put, when both belong to the same animal category, the score is the maximum, namely 2. Score 1 is given for the following combinations:

- Bride - human, groom - chatuspada
- Bride - jalchar, groom - chatuspada
- Bride - Keet, groom - chatuspada
- Bride - Chatuspada, Groom human
- Bride - Keet, Groom - human
- Bride - Chatuspada, Groom - Jalchar
- Bride - Keet, Groom - Keet
- Bride - Jalchar, Groom - Vanacara
- Bride - Chatuspada, Groom - Keet
- Bride - Human, Groom - Keet
- Bride - Jalchar, Groom - Keet

Score 1.5 is given for the following combinations:

- Bride - Jalchar, Groom - Human
- Bride - Human, Groom - Jalchar
- Bride - Chatuspada, Groom - Vanacara

Score 0 is given for the following combinations:

- Bride - Vanacara, Groom - Chatuspada
- Bride - Vanacara, Groom - human
- Bride - Vanacara, Groom - jalchar
- Bride - Keet, Groom - Vanacara
- Bride - Vanacara, Groom - Keet
- Bride - human, Groom - Vanacara

Tara Koot - This category determines the overall destiny and well-being of the prospective couple. The 27 Nakshatras are divided into nine groups. Studying the bride's and groom's stars within the framework of this division is a good indicator of the marriage's success. Starting from the bride's star, count until the boy's Nakshatra is reached. Divide this number by 9; the remainder reflects the overall well-being of the couple. The remainder is matched against the nine life aspects discussed in the previous chapter. They are:

1. Janma - Bad
2. Sampath - Good
3. Vipat - Bad
4. Kshema - Good
5. Prayatak - Bad
6. Sadhana - Good
7. Vadha or Naidhana - Bad
8. Mitra - Good
9. Parama Mitra - Good

For example, if the count from the girl's star to the boy's star is 12, dividing 12 by 9 gets you a quotient of 1 and a remainder of 3. Now, 3 represents Vipat, which is bad, and therefore, the Tara Koot indicator is not good for the marriage.

Yoni Koot - The matching of this prospective couple's aspect is the most popular in matching horoscopes for marriages. This Koot stands for the sexual energy and attraction between the girl and boy. Nakshatras are given animal symbols that reflect each asterism's sexual behavior. The sexual compatibility is achieved by comparing the animals projected by both the girl's and boy's birth stars.

The five animals include:

1. Swabhava Yoni
2. Friend or Mitra Yoni
3. Neutral Yoni
4. Opposite Yoni
5. Enemy Yoni

The sexual compatibility is the best in the Swabhava Yoni pair because both the bride and the groom share the same class of Yoni. It is easy to understand that the least compatible pair is the Enemy pair because each of the partners belongs to an entirely different yoni class. Now, look at the classification of Nakshatras based on Yoni and use examples to explain the pairs:

- Ashwini and Shatabhisha belong to the Ashwa (horse) class of Yoni
- Bharani and Revati belong to the Gaja (elephant) class of Yoni
- Pushya and Kritika belong to the Mesha (sheep) class of Yoni
- Rohini and Mrigashirsha belong to the Sarpa (serpent) class of Yoni
- Moola and Ardra belong to the Shwan (dog) class of Yoni
- Ashlesha and Punarvasu belong to the Marjara (cat) class of Yoni
- Magha and Purva Phalguni belong to the Mushaka (rat) class of Yoni
- Uttara Phalguni and Uttara Bhadrapada belong to the Gau (cow) class of Yoni
- Swati and Hasta belong to the Mahisha (buffalo) class of Yoni
- Vishakha and Chitra belong to the Vyaghra (tiger) class of Yoni
- Jyeshtha and Anuradha belong to the Mriga (deer) class of Yoni
- Purvashada and Shravana belong to the Vanara (monkey) class of Yoni

- Uttarashada and Abhijeet belong to the Nakul (mongoose) class of Yoni

- Purva Bhadrapada and Dhanishta belong to the Singha (lion) class of Yoni

Natives belonging to the same class of Yoni are sexually more compatible than natives belonging to different classes. For example, if the bride and groom are of Moola and Ashlesha Nakshatra, respectively, their Yoni classes would be dog and cat, which are natural enemies. Therefore, their sexual compatibility from their horoscopes' point of view will not be good at all.

Graha-Maitri Koot – This element in the Ashtakoot Guna Milan system is used to determine the mutual love and respect and mentality of a prospective couple. This element is also a measure of the partners' willingness to work together to make the marriage successful. This element's score will help you determine whether you and your prospective spouse will agree with each other more or disagree.

This aspect is studied in detail by reading into the planet lords of the prospective bride's and groom's Zodiac signs. If the Rashis of the bride and groom are ruled by friendly planets and belong to the same Moon sign, the pair is expected to be highly compassionate and understanding of each other.

Contrarily, if enemy planets rule the Zodiac signs of the bride and the groom, this element's score will be low, and the marriage would not be an approachable one. The maximum points for this element are 6.

Gana Koot – This element determines the basic characteristic of a person. Nakshatras are divided into three categories, namely Devta, Manushya, and Rakshasa Gana. These categories represent three different natures or behavioral attitudes of the native. For example, a person from the Devta Gana would be patient and gentle in their behavior. An individual from the Rakshasa Gana would be inconsiderate, rude, aggressive, but straightforward. A person from the

Manushya Gana would be somewhere between these two. They would be gentle but ready to become aggressive if the situation demanded it. Here are the Nakshatras and their respective Ganas:

- Devta Gana - Ashwini, Mrigashirsha, Punarvasu, Pushya, Hasta, Swati, Anuradha, Shravana, and Revati

- Manushya Gana - Bharani, Rohini, Ardra, Purva Phalguni, Uttara Phalguni, Purvashada, Uttarashada, Purva Bhadrapada, and Uttara Bhadrapada

- Rakshasa Gana - Krittika, Ashlesha, Magha, Chitra, Vishakha, Jyeshtha, Moola, Dhanishta, and Satabhisha

Bhakoot Koot - Also referred to as Rashi Koot, this element of the Ashtakoot Guna Milan system is allocated 7 points. The moon signs, and the placement of Chandra in the Rashi Charts of the prospective couple, are taken into consideration for this Koot. These two aspects are analyzed and evaluated for their strengths and weaknesses.

If the bride and groom's birth sign is 6-8, Shadashtak Yoga is considered to be formed. In this Yoga, if the planet lords of the two Moon signs are natural enemies, the marital life is likely to be full of problems and sufferings. Financial problems, accidents, and problems from direct and indirect enemies are likely to bring suffering to the married couple.

Dwidwadash dosha is when a combination of 2-12 is obtained when comparing the bride's and groom's birth signs. If the combination is 5-9, Navapancham Dosha is formed. The Navapancham Dosha makes the groom have a sense of detachment from the real world.

Contrarily, if the bride's moon sign is 9 when counted from the groom's moon sign, the bride might tend to abandon the world. However, if the planets of both moon signs are friendly, this situation could settle down.

Full points, 7, is given if the bride's and groom's Moon signs are the same or if the moon of both is on the 1/7, 3/11, and 4/10 axes. This Guna gets 0 points if the moon is on the 2/12, 5/9, and 6/8 axis.

Nadi Koot – The 27 Nakshatras are categorized into three types, namely Aadi, Madhya, and Antya Nadi. These are collectively called Nadi Milan or Nadi Dosha. With 8 points, this Koot is an important element to consider for matching the horoscopes of the bride and groom.

Nadi should be different for the bride and groom for the horoscopes to get a go-ahead for marriage. If they are the same, the marriage will not be a good one because the children of this marriage could suffer from health problems. While the same Nadi couples should not be considered for marriage, if the Nakshatras of the bride and groom are different, the same Nadi can be considered. Matching Nadi Koot is a complex and layered process.

According to Vedic Astrology, a marriage between a bride and groom, both belonging to Devta Gana Nakshatras, would be highly auspicious. A marriage between a groom from the Rakshasa Gana and a bride from the Devta Gana would be very inauspicious and unstable. Ideally, people from the same Gana should be chosen as partners.

Lastly, while the Ashtakoot Guna Milan score gives a reasonable, clear picture of marriage prospects, it is not sufficient by itself. Other astrological factors should also be considered before arriving at a final decision. Expert astrologers believe that the scores can be taken as a good indicator but should never be taken in isolation. The other factors to be considered along with the Ashtakoot Guna Milan scores include:

- The Lagna of the bride and groom
- The strength of the ascendant and that of its ruler
- The strength of the seventh house and its ruler
- The strength and nature of Jupiter and Venus

- The natural friendship/relationship between the rulers of the Lagna and the seventh house
- All the Nakshatra positions that deal with mental, physical, and financial compatibility of the bride and groom

Venus specifically requires special attention because this planet's strength and weakness play an important role in a marriage's success or failure. Inauspicious placement of Venus in the boy's horoscope can cause infertility. In a girl's horoscope, Jupiter plays a crucial because it reflects the house of the husband. Its strength and weakness can be a good indicator of the future of marriage.

You can also see how Nakshatras and other aspects of Vedic Astrology can help you determine a good partner for yourself. The next chapter deals with career planning.

Chapter 8: Nakshatras and Career Planning

Career Planning is another important topic in Predictive Vedic Astrology. Career planning is a crucial aspect of life, and Vedic Astrology can be a highly useful tool to see the direction and path that your career is likely to take. The native's Nakshatra and its lord are powerful indicators of the career path. Now, look at each of the Nakshatras and their inspiration toward natives' professions.

Ashwini – the Star of Transport

Ashwini, located in Mesha Rashi and ruled by Ketu, is known as the Star of Transport. Ketu renders a mystical and mysterious aura to the life journey of a native born in Ashwini. The symbol of this asterism, a horse's head, is a powerful indicator of the adventurous spirit combined with a headstrong personality of Ashwini natives.

The ruling gods are the Ashwin twins, who ride in a golden chariot showering healing power to Earth's mortals. The Ashwin twins are referred to as the "Physicians to the Gods." Their healing and revitalizing powers form the crux of their strength. They heal people and help them reach their goals and achieve their dreams.

Ashwini Nakshatra has a Devata Guna (godly temperament), and they are motivated by dharma. The career interests of natives born in Ashwini Nakshatra are usually:

- Therapists and psychologists
- Mystic healers and physicians
- Law enforcement agency workers, including military
- Travel agents and other travel and transportation-related jobs
- Athletes, jockeys, and horse trainers

Bharani – the Star of Restraint

Covered by the Aries Zodiac, Bharani Nakshatra is ruled by Venus or Shukra. The symbol is a yoni or clay vessel. This symbol reflects Bharani's potent creative energy, considering it is ruled by Venus, the representative power of sexual energy and creativity.

The ruling deity is Yama, the Lord of Death. Interestingly, in the Atharva Veda, Bharani is listed as the last Nakshatra, symbolizing the end of things and life. Bharani is also known as Apabharani, which translates to "water that carries away things."

This power symbolizes the potential to remove and cleanse impurities. With a manushya temperament, Bharani's primary motive is prosperity or artha (wealth). The career interests of Bharani-born natives are:

- Writers, publishers, and jobs in the film and music industry
- Occultists, hypnotists, astrologers, and psychologists
- Business entrepreneurs, building contractors, and financial consultants
- Careers and jobs in the hotel industry, including catering, chef, etc.

- Careers related to births and deaths, such as fertility specialists, morticians, workers in funeral homes, and gynecologists.
- Politicians, lawyers, and judges

Krittika – the Star of Fire

Ruled by Surya, and with Agni (the Lord of Fire) as the ruling deity, Krittika's symbol is the primordial flame, representing purification through yagna or the sacrificial fire. This Nakshatra's power is to "burn away" ignorance and negativity to reveal the underlying truth. It has a Rakshasa nature, and the primary motive is desire or kama. The career interests of Krittika-born natives are:

- Heads of states, advisors, and spiritual teachers
- Fashion designers, models, musicians, artists, singers, and dancers
- Weapon makers, military personnel, and building contractors
- Potters, cooks, Vedic priests, and other professions involving fire

Rohini – the Star of Ascent

Chandra rules Rohini, and the ruling deity is Brahman, the creator. Rohini has many symbols, including a temple, chariot, and banyan tree. This Nakshatra's power represents a movement toward the divine (temple). The banyan tree is considered sacred and the home of the Goddesses of the Indus Valley Civilization. With a manushya temperament, the primary motivation for Rohini is spiritual liberation. Careers for Rohini natives are:

- Models, actors, and fashion designers
- High positions in the hotel industry

- Careers in food products, agriculture, real estate, and herbal market
- Consultants and politicians

Mrigashirsha – the Searching Star

Mrigashirsha is ruled by Mars and has the symbol of a deer's face. This Nakshatra has a devta temperament, and spiritual liberation is the primary motivation. Mars, its ruling planet, represents the energy of a spiritual warrior. This is a great constellation for research of philosophical and spiritual pursuits. Careers of Mrigashirsha natives include:

- Teachers, researchers, actors, writers, and poets
- Mystics, astrologers, and psychics
- Gemologists and engineers
- Animal trainers and veterinary doctors
- Careers in the travel industry, real estate, and business development

Ardra – the Star of Sorrow

The main symbol of Ardra is a human head. It is ruled by Rahu, who represents thinking. The second symbol of Ardra is a teardrop, which reflects the power to overcome suffering. Ardra is a Nakshatra associated with brilliant mental ability and represents emotional cleansing that happens after suffering. Ardra career interests include:

- Careers in hospitals, hospice cares, and pain management
- Teachers, writers, social service workers, and public relations
- Careers in humanitarian projects and politics
- Mathematics, atomic research, and engineering
- Drug dealers, butchers, chemists

Punarvasu – the Star of Renewal

This illuminating asterism has a bow and a quiver of arrows as its symbol. The meaning of Punarvasu is "the return of the light." This star's power lies in its ability to restore the light of spirituality into the darkness of ignorance. It also stands for moral values, purity, and truth. The strength of this Nakshatra is the ability to gain abundance and wealth. Punarvasu is ruled by Jupiter, the greatest of benefic planets. Career interests include:

- Careers in the entertainment industry, including acting, drama, etc.
- Directors, publishers, and writers
- Psychologists, mystics, spiritual teachers, and philosophers
- Civil engineers, architects, inventors, and scientists
- Social workers and politicians

Pushya – the Star of Nourishment

Pushya is considered to be the most auspicious Nakshatras among all the 27. It has various symbols, including a circle, lotus, arrow, and, most particularly, a cow's udder. With a deva temperament, the primary motivation for Pushya is dharma, or rightful action and living. Saturn, its ruling planet, offers stable grounding for this asterism. The power of Pushya is the ability to create spiritual energy. Career interests include:

- Careers in politics and governments
- Careers in the police, military, and law
- Artists, poets, and musicians
- Careers in the dairy industry and geology
- Spiritual and religious teachers

Ashlesha – the Clinging Star

A coiled serpent is the symbol of this intense asterism. The coiled serpent represents the immense potential of Kundalini energy residing at the base of the spine. Ashlesha translates to "entwine" and denotes the challenges of human beings to be excessively attached to sensory and materialistic pleasures. The power of Ashlesha is the ability to spout venom. With a Rakshasa temperament, people born in Ashlesha Nakshatra are driven by dharma. Career interests are:

- Teachers, writers, lawyers
- Zoologists and other animal-related studies
- Mystics, astrologers, and psychics
- Careers in business development and speculative ventures, including the stock market
- Chemists, drug dealers, gamblers
- Addiction counselors and sex therapists

Magha – the Star of Power

Magha means "the mighty one." This asterism stands for strength and spiritual leadership. Ruled by Ketu, Magha's symbol, which has a Rakshasa temperament, is the king's palanquin or bed. The primary motivation of people born under Magha is material prosperity or artha. The power of Magha is "the ability to leave the body." Career interests include:

- Business entrepreneurs and self-employment
- Researchers, historians, and archeologists
- Careers in the field of drama and cinema
- Heads of corporations, lawyers, and politicians

Purva Phalguni – the Fruit of the Tree

Purva Phalguni is ruled by Venus and is known for its creative power. People born in this sign are usually skilled in the fine arts and love pleasurable pursuits driven by their primary motivation, namely kama or desire. The symbol of this asterism is a couch, swinging hammock, or two legs of a bed – all three reflect a place and time of enjoyment and rest. Purva Phalguni has a manushya temperament and is known for "the power of creative procreation." Career interests include:

- Careers in photography, radio, and television
- Artists, musicians, actors, and models
- Travel agents and careers in retail sales
- Wedding planners and jobs in jewelry and cosmetics
- Politicians and government service
- Marital and sex therapists

Uttara Phalguni – the Star of Patronage

The symbol of this asterism is a healing bed or the two legs of a cot. It is a service-oriented Nakshatra and is ever ready to help a friend in need. Uttara Phalguni star people possess excellent healing skills and can find harmony in careers related to healing and counseling. With a manushya temperament, the main motivation for this asterism is spiritual liberation. The power of Uttara Phalguni is "the ability to give prosperity through marriage." Career interests include:

- Philanthropists, social workers, and careers in charitable work
- State health officials and careers in the healing art
- Actors, writers, and media personnel
- Mathematicians, astrologers, and astronomers

- Business entrepreneurs and jobs in public relations and sales

Hasta

The symbol of Hasta Nakshatra is the hand or palm. The ruling deity is Savitar, the creative form of Surya. The power of Hasta is "the capability to manifest what the seeker seeks and put it in their hands." Hasta natives are known for excellent dexterity with their hands and are good with handicrafts and healing arts. With a devta temperament, the primary motivation of Hasta Nakshatra is spiritual liberation. Career interests include:

- Artists, painters, and craftsmen
- Teachers, scholars, performers, comedians, and writers
- Careers in voluntary work and hospitals.
- Careers in public relations
- Ministers, advisers, psychotherapists, and counselors
- Careers in networking and communication
- Conference planners and travel-related jobs

Chitra – the Star of Opportunity

Chitra means "the beautiful one," and its symbol is a pearl or bright jewel. The power of this asterism is the "ability to organize and arrange things aesthetically and artistically." The power of this Nakshatra is also "to accumulate good karma." With a rakshasa nature, the primary motivation for Chitra Nakshatra is kama. Career interests of Chitra Nakshatra are:

- Jewelers, clothing and fashion designers
- Interior designers and architects
- Judges, lawyers, priests

- Careers in religious fields related to the knowledge of scriptures
- Careers in creative business and the field of art and music
- Writers, publishers, TV, films, and radio

Swati – the Self-Motivated Star

Ruled by Rahu, the symbol for Swati Nakshatra is a single blade of grass blowing in the wind. This symbol reflects the autonomous and independent nature of this constellation. People born in this star love traveling for education and learning. They are always yearning to make positive changes. Swati's primary power is its "capability to scatter things in the wind," considering its ruling deity is Vayu, the Wind God. With a devta temperament, another symbol for Swati is a sword reflecting the power of accurate discrimination. Career interests include:

- Entrepreneurs and independent business owners
- Positions of leadership
- Careers in sales, travel, and the transportation industry
- Meditation and yoga teachers
- Careers in the legal profession, including lawyers, judges, etc.
- Drug and alcohol traders, stockbrokers

Vishakha – the Star of Purpose

Jupiter rules Vishakha, and its ruling deity is Agni. The power of this Nakshatra is its "ability to obtain different fruits in life." The symbol is an archway or a potter's wheel. The archway represents the threshold of a spiritual journey. The potter's wheel is a reflection of the patience needed to succeed in the spiritual path. Career interests are:

- Public speakers, teachers, writers
- Scientists and researchers
- Lawyers and politicians
- Dictators, military leaders
- Ambassadors of humanitarian work

Anuradha – the Star of Success

The ruling planet of Anuradha is Saturn, which gives discipline and tenacity during difficult times. Its symbol is a lotus, which reflects its capability to blossom regardless of the external circumstances. Its ruling deity is Mitra, the Lord of Partnership and Friendship. People born in this Nakshatra are skilled at gathering people together for both social and spiritual activities.

With a devta temperament, the primary motivation of Anuradha Nakshatra is dharma. Its primary power lies in the "ability to worship." Career interests include:

- Careers in business management
- Planners and organizers
- Careers in the travel industry
- Public speakers, musicians, and actors
- Plumbers and mining engineers
- Politicians and criminal lawyers

Jyeshta – the Elder or Chief Star

Jyeshtha translates to "senior-most" or "eldest." The symbols for this asterism are an umbrella and earring. The latter represents Lord Vishnu's discus, while the umbrella symbolizes status and protection. Jyeshtha has a rakshasa nature, and its primary motivation is the accumulation of wealth. The power of this constellation is its "ability to rise and conquer in battle through courage and bravery." Career interests include:

- Business managers and self-employment
- Dancers, musicians, and models
- Philosophers, researchers, and intellectuals
- Police detectives and military leaders
- Engineers and careers in exploration and mining

Moola – the Foundation Star

Moola means "the root or foundation." Its symbol is a bunch of roots tied together. The ruling planet is Ketu, which reflects a sense of mysticism to this constellation. The ruling deity is Nirritti, the Goddess of Destruction, connected to Kali, the all-powerful destroyer of evil. The power of Moola is the "ability to destroy, ruin, and break things." It is a rakshasa Nakshatra, and its primary motivation is Kama. Career interests include:

- Spiritual teachers, philosophers, and ministers
- Writers and public speakers
- Politicians and lawyers
- Business entrepreneurs
- Careers in sales
- Healers, doctors, and pharmacists

Purvashada – the Invincible Star

Purvashada translates to "early victory" or the "undefeated." Ruled by Venus, the symbol of this asterism is a winnowing basket or fan that can rid the corn from its husk. The ruling deity is Apas, the Cosmic Waters. The power of this Nakshatra is in its capability to invigorate. With a manushya temperament, the primary motivation of Purvashada is spiritual liberation. Career interests are:

- Careers in the boating and shipping industry
- Debaters, teachers, writers, and public speakers
- Careers in foreign trade and travel industry
- Careers in the film industry as actors and directors
- Politicians and lawyers

Uttarashada – the Universal Star

The meaning of Uttarashada is "later victory." Its symbol is an elephant tusk associated with Lord Ganesha, the remover of obstacles. It has a second symbol, the planks of a bed, which signifies peace, rest, and security. Uttarashada has a manushya temperament, and its primary motivation is spiritual liberation. The power of this asterism is "the ability for unchallengeable victory." Career interests include:

- Social workers and government servants
- Innovators and pioneers
- Researchers, healers, and scientists
- Hunters and careers in the military
- Fighters who fight for a cause

Shravana – the Star of Learning

Shravana means "to listen," and therefore, its primary symbol is an ear. With a devta temperament, Shravana's power is in its ability to hear the astral sounds from Lord Krishna's flute, the cosmic Om, and the celestial bells. People born in this star usually have brilliant minds and can easily study other cultures and spiritual dimensions. Their primary motivation is the creation of wealth. Career interests include:

- Speech therapists, teachers, and linguists
- Religious priests, scholars, and astrologers
- Careers in business, politics, geology
- Researchers and professors
- Careers in the travel industry

Dhanishta – the Star of Symphony

Also referred to as the "kingly star," people under the influence of Dhanishta can earn much fame and wealth. Its symbol is the drum, which reflects a love for music. With a rakshasa temperament, people born in this asterism are likely to be challenged by a fiery temper and marriage difficulties. Career interests include:

- Drummers, poets, and musicians
- Surgeons and doctors
- Careers in property management and real estate
- Careers in mining and engineering
- Researchers and scientists
- Careers in humanitarian work and charitable projects

Shatabisha - the Hundred Stars

Shatabisha also translates to "the hundred flowers" or "the hundred healers." Its symbol is an empty circle, which reflects an independent and autonomous character. The ruling deity is Varuna, the God of Water and Medicine, which is why natives born in this asterism have a strong connection to the healing arts. The power of Shatabisha is "the ability to heal." Shatabisha has a Rakshasa temperament, and its primary motivation is dharma or rightful action. Career interests are:

- Astronomers and astrologers
- Nurses, physicians, and healers
- Researchers, writers, and nuclear scientists
- Careers in the clerical industry, including secretaries and editors
- Electricians and engineers
- Careers in organizational capacities and business skills

Purva Bhadrapada – the Burning Pair

This asterism has three symbols: a two-faced man, the front two legs of a funeral cot, and a sword. The two-faced man and the two legs represent the power of the natives born in this asterism to see both sides of an issue. The sword represents the power to slice through negativity to get to the ultimate truth. The primary power of Purva Bhadrapada is "the ability to lift an individual in his or her spiritual life." With a manushya temperament, the primary motivation for these asterisms is the accumulation of wealth. Career interests include:

- Careers in business and administration
- Researchers and statisticians
- Ascetics, priests, and idealistic visionaries
- Occultists, astrologers, tantric

- Careers in geriatric field, hospice work, and nursing

Uttara Bhadrapada – the Warrior Star

The symbol of the Uttara Bhadrapada is represented by the back two legs of a funeral cot. Another symbol is a pair of twins. The word "Bhadrapada" means "scorching" or "burning pair." It connects the twin Nakshatras of Purva and Uttara Bhadrapada. With a manushya temperament, the primary motivation for this asterism is a pleasure. Career interests include:

- Careers in non-profit and charitable organizations
- Careers in the travel industry and import-export
- Saints, religious careers like priests and priestess, mystics, and astrologers
- Philosophers, writers, researchers, and teachers

Revati – the Wealthy Star

The symbols for Revati are a drum and fish. The drum is a marker of time signifying the last constellation in the Zodiac. The fish represents deep spirituality. This Nakshatra has a devta temperament, and the primary motivation is spiritual liberation. The power of Revati is "the power to nourish." Revati is considered one of the most beneficial asterisms for developing psychic abilities and spiritual growth. Career interests include:

- Careers in charitable and humanitarian causes
- Animal trainers and vets
- Publishers, editors, and journalists
- Government services, social work, and urban planners
- Careers in the travel industry, including flight attendants

In Vedic Astrology, every aspect of life, including careers, can be determined by reading deeply into the native's divisional charts. Unlike Western Astrology, which only looks at the Zodiac sign of an individual to predict career paths, Vedic Astrology covers a wide horizon of factors that affect this aspect of your life.

Your Nakshatra, the symbols they represent, the ruling deities, the ruling planets, the positional aspect of the planets to each other—both on the Zodiac and on the concerned individual's divisional charts—and many more determinants are taken into account to find the right bill in terms of career. In comparison, methods used by Western Astrology appear insufficient and superficial.

The indicators given in this chapter are only a form of guidance. Feel free to consult a reputed astrologer and seek help if you want to delve into your career-changing plans. Having a strong basic idea will help you understand your life's career path even as you seek a professional's guidance.

Chapter 9: The Muhurta: Electional Astrology

Muhurta or Electional Astrology—also known as event astrology—is based on the concept of Nakshatras and involves determining what the best time for an event is based on the astrological auspiciousness of that time. It plays an important part in all Indian households because the start of any crucial event sets the pace for the event's success or failure. Again, Nakshatras and its various connected aspects, including directions, natures, and others, fix auspicious times for events—a topic referred to as Electional Astrology.

Understanding the Concept of Muhurta

Muhurta has multiple connotations and definitions. Interestingly, Abhijeet Nakshatra—the 28th one that is not considered for other aspects of predictive astrology—plays an important role in Muhurtha. Read on to learn more.

Muhurta is a measure of time used in Hindu calendars. The duration of a muhurta is 48 minutes counted from the time of sunrise. It is important to note here that according to the Hindu calendar known as Panchanga System, a day of 24 hours is measured from sunrise to sunrise and not from midnight.

The smallest time unit known to ancient India's seers is called a "Nimisha," which is considered the smallest unit of time conceivable by human beings. "Nimisha" is defined as "the blink of an eye." This is a linear concept and a fixed measure. The bigger measurements of time are:

- Fifteen nimisha equals one kashta
- Fifteen kashta equals one laghu
- Fifteen laghu equals one ghatika (another name for ghatika is "danda")
- Two ghatika (or 30 laghu) equals one muhurta
- 30 muhurta equals one divai-ratri (24 hours)

Astrologically, one muhurta is not taken exactly as 48 minutes every day. This value varies depending on the local moon, sunrise, and sunset. It is a non-linear, cyclical concept, and therefore, is not fixed. One sidereal day and night—referred to as "nakshatra ahoratra"—has 30 muhurtas. Each sidereal day and night is divided into four time zones—called Praharas, each of seven and one-third muhurtas—as follows:

- The time between sunrise and noon is the first Prahara
- The time between noon and sunset is the second Prahara
- The time between sunset and midnight is the third Prahara
- The time between midnight and the next sunrise is the fourth Prahara

The four points in time, namely sunrise, noon, sunset, and midnight are called Gayatri pada. Therefore, four Praharas make 24 hours. The Abhijeet Muhurta, which is the last half Muhurta in the first Prahara and the first half Muhurta in the second Prahara, is considered very auspicious as it is mapped to the Abhijeet Nakshatra ruled by Lord Hari.

The seven Nakshatras before Abhijeet, namely Swati, Vishakha, Anuradha, Jyeshtha, Magha, Purva Phalguni, and Uttara Phalguni, constitute the remaining seven Muhurtas in the first Prahara. The balance of twenty Nakshatras then fits into the twenty Muhurtas of the remaining three Praharas after the Abhijeet Muhurta. Thus, all the 28 Nakshatra fit into the 28 Muhurtas of each day. The remaining two Muhurtas of the day—totaling 96 minutes before sunrise—are attributed to the God of Creation, Brahma, and, therefore, is loosely referred to as Brahma Muhurta.

However, the last two Muhurtas have different energies and are better associated with different deities. The 29th—the second last one—is attributed to Brahma, and the last one belongs to Surya, or Savitur, the Sun God's creative form. Lord Brahma is the ruling deity of Saturn and is related to the rebirth of the soul, which is why the 29th Brahma Muhurta is great to meditate on your Creator.

The last Muhurta is excellent for seeking the blessings of Savitur to direct your intelligence to the correct path. Each of the other Muhurtas of the day has its own significance.

Selection of the Muhurta

The following factors are taken into consideration during Muhurta selection, which consists of the day and time to undertake events:

- The tithi (or the Lunar Day)
- Nakshatra (the asterism in which Chandra is placed on that day)
- The Yoga Karana (or the auspiciousness of the chosen time)
- Vara (the weekday)

In addition to the above, certain times during the day are considered good/bad, and certain combinations of Nakshatras and weekdays are considered good/bad, etc. These considerations also need to be taken into account before selecting the Muhurta.

The Thithi

There are 30 thithis in a lunar month divided into two fortnights, each starting from the new moon day and the full moon day. In addition to being the lunar date, a thithi is a measure of the Sun and Moon's separation. Each Thithi has its own planetary lord, and people born in different thithis have varying characteristics. For example, a person born on the full moon day (Poornima) has stronger characteristic traits than one born on a new moon day (amavasya). The thithis are divided into five types:

1. **Ananda (Joyous) Thithis** - Prathipada (the first day of the fortnight), Shasti (the sixth day), and Ekadashi (the eleventh day) form the full moon or amavasya day. These days bestow joy and happiness.

2. **Mangala Thithis** - Also known as Bhadra, Arogya, or healthy thithis, these include Dwitiya (the second day), Saptami (the seventh day), and Dwadashi (the twelfth day). These days are good for starting new work.

3. **Jaya Thithis** - Jaya means victory, and the days include Tritiya (the third day of a fortnight) that falls on a Tuesday, Ashtami (the eighth day), and Trayodashi (the thirteenth day). These days are good for winning over rivals and enemies.

4. **Rikkta Thithis** - Also known as Nashta or Loss thithis, these lunar days include Chaturthi (the fourth day) falling on a Saturday, Navami (the ninth day), and Chaturdashi (the fourteenth day). These days are not good to undertake any important work or event -they should be completely avoided.

5. **Poorna Thithis** - Also known as Sampoorna days, these thithis include Panchami (the fifth day falling on a Thursday), Dashami (the tenth day), and Amavasya or Poornima (the fifteenth day of the fortnight). These are good for doing all activities.

Additionally, times such as Rahukalam, Gulika Kalam, and Yamagandam that happen every day should be avoided while fixing the Muhurta for auspicious events. The days of the week (Vara) have their important elements to consider. Now, look at them in more detail.

Vara or Weekday

Sunday - Sunday is known as Adivaram and Bhanuvaram as it is related to the Sun God, Surya, who is also known as Aditya. Adivaram is a day of life and a day filled with pure consciousness. It is a day to enjoy life, the power of the sun, and focus on the inner self. Sunday is a good day for work related to gold, trees, copper, nature, fire, silk, and coronation. On this day, controlling your temper and ego yields good karma, and it is also important not to be rude or lazy.

Monday - Known as Somavaram, this day is dedicated to the Moon or Chandra. It is a day of original thinking, creativity, and intuition. It's good for purchasing new items, including jewelry, clothes, and others. It's also a good day to conduct marriages, make intuitive decisions, and make changes with elements related to your mother, milk, and water. It's important not to be rigid and tough on Mondays. Moreover, it's not good for hair cutting, a manicure, and other barber- or parlor-related activities.

Tuesday - Tuesday or Mangalvaram is dedicated to Mars or Mangala. It is a day for material things and good for work related to metals, minerals, fire, medicine, sporting activities, and electricity. It's not a good day to start new things. It's better to avoid traveling on Tuesdays. You must take care and beware of quarrels, injuries, accidents, and falls on Tuesdays.

Wednesday - Known as Bhuddhavaram, it is a day dedicated to Mercury or Bhuddh. It's a day of knowledge, wisdom, and happiness. It's a good day for all kinds of refined work, including sales, business, shopping, starting new projects, communicating, gaining knowledge, taking medicines, marriages, and more. It's best if you avoid lying and being cruel and violent on Wednesdays.

Thursday – Called Guruvaram, according to the Vedic Calendar, Thursday is dedicated to Jupiter or Guru. It is a day of knowledge, wisdom, devotion, money, and children. It's a highly favorable day for all kinds of activities such as marriages, charitable work, gifts, shopping for important things, trading, planning finances, and starting new things in your life. You must not get angry, be greedy, lazy, or violent on Thursdays.

Friday – Friday or Shukravaram is dedicated to Venus or Shukra. It is a day of pleasures, love, harmony, fine arts, happiness, and good fortune. It's good for purchasing clothes, accessories, including jewelry, marriages, inviting and visiting friends and family, and everything else. Avoid selling important items you own on this day and being lonely.

Saturday – Dedicated to Saturn or Shani, Saturday is known as Shanivaram. It is a day of rest and recovery. It's a day for service work and charity. Taking rest on Saturdays is considered good for longevity. It's not a good day to begin anything new. It's a good day to do activities related to housing, farming, meditation, and yoga. Do not create a fuss and be careful about your health. Avoid barber- and parlor-related activities on Saturdays.

Timing of Events and 27 Nakshatras

Rohini, Uttarashadha, Uttara Bhadrapada, and Uttara Phalguni are fixed constellations, and therefore, favorable asterisms for activities with long-term, sustained, and permanent effects including:

- Digging wells
- Laying the foundations of homes, commercial establishments, temples, and even towns and cities
- Planting trees
- Purchasing land and property

- Doing meritorious deeds
- Sowing seeds
- Deity installations

Revati, Anuradha, Chitra, and Mrigashirsha are considered gentle and soft Nakshatras, and therefore, auspicious for the following activities:

- Beginning lessons in new subjects
- Fine arts, including singing, dancing
- Making new friendships and partnerships
- For sensual pleasures, including sexual union
- Wearing new clothes
- Taking out processions
- Conducting auspicious ceremonies
- Festivities
- To undertake journeys
- For agricultural activities

Hasta, Pushya, and Ashwini Nakshatras are considered to be light and swift, and so are good for the following activities:

- Sports and exercises
- Enjoying luxurious items
- Starting new industries
- Skilled labor-related jobs
- Medical treatments
- For starting education and journeys
- Seeing and meeting friends
- Buying and selling
- To perform spiritual activities

- Fine arts-related activities
- Giving and receiving loans

Satabhisha, Swati, Punarvasu, Shravana, and Dhanishta are movable and quick asterisms, and therefore, suitable for the following activities of a temporary nature:

- Undertaking journeys and travels
- Buying vehicles
- Gardening
- Processions
- Visiting friends

Purva Bhadrapada, Purvashada, Purva Phalguni, and Bharani are cruel and fierce Nakshatras. They are good for indulging in acts of deceit and evil, including:

- Conflicts and battles
- Destructions of rivals and enemies
- Incarceration
- Poisoning
- Arson
- Activities of ill-repute

Vishakha and Krittika are mixed Nakshatras and suitable for routine activities, including those related to your home and office.

How to Find an Auspicious Muhurta

There are some very broad guidelines you can use to find an auspicious time on your own. Here is a brief explanation. You can see any Panchang and check for these details.

Thithis - Avoid Chaturdashi (fourteenth day), Dwadashi (the twelfth day, but some days are fine), Navami (the ninth day), Ashtami (the eighth day), Shasti (the sixth day), and Chaturthi (the fourth day)

Varas - Monday (Somavaram), Wednesday (Bhuddhavaram), Thursday (Guruvaram), and Friday (Shukravaram) are the best, while Tuesday (Mangalavaram), Saturday (Shanivaram), and Sunday (Adivaram) are to be avoided.

Nakshatras - Those with a downward-looking direction should be avoided. These asterisms, including Bharani, Krittika, Ashlesha, Magha, Purva Phalguni, Vishakha, Moola, Purvashada, and Purva Bhadrapada, are to be avoided while fixing Muhurtas.

Yogas - There are 27 different Panchanga Yogas defined in Vedic Astrology. The ones to be avoided for auspicious occasions are Vishakumbha, Shoola, Atigandam, Gandam, Vaidhruti, Vyatipaatam, Vajram, Parigham, and Vyaghaatam.

Karana - This stands for half lunar days, and there are eleven of them defined in the Hindu Panchanga System. The ones to avoid for auspicious occasions are Chatuspadam, Vishti, Kimstughnam, Shakunam, and Nagam.

Note that the elements discussed in Chapter 2, which deal with the nature, direction, and other elements of a Nakshatra, are employed to arrive at fixing Muhurtas for auspicious events.

Chapter 10: The K.P. System of Stellar Astrology

This bonus chapter introduces you to a new system of Astrology known as K.P. Astrology. Although derived from Vedic Astrology, the K P System is focused on the use of Nakshatras and their Cuspal Lords. Read on to find out more about this intriguing system of Nakshatra-based Vedic Astrology.

The K. P. System of Stellar Astrology got its name from its inventor, Professor Kuthur Subbarayaiyyer Krishnamurthi, who lived from 1908 to 1972. He developed this new technique of making astrological predictions, which are based on the sub-lords. The K.P. System is based on the Stellar System of predictions.

The stellar astrology system was significantly researched by Shri Gopalakrishna Rao (famously known as Meena I) and N. V. Raghava Chary (known as Meena II). This system subdivides the 27 Nakshatras into 243 parts to indicate something called the asterisms' Kaalamsa positions. Professor Krishnamurthi knew both these stalwarts intimately.

He extended the theory after working on it for numerous years and brought in further divisions. According to Professor Krishnamurthi, the twelve bhavas or houses or lordship positions are subdivided into 249 positions of sub-lord. He employed the unequal proportion of the Vimshottari Dasa System to create these subdivisions.

It is important to note that Professor Krishnamurti did not go against the grain of the traditional form of Vedic Astrology. In fact, he emphasizes the importance of getting the fundamentals of the ancient system perfectly right before venturing into the K. P. System of Stellar Astrology. Some deviations from the traditional Vedic Astrology system have been taken by the founders of K. P. System, summarized as follows.

To reiterate, there are twelve Zodiac Signs (or Rashis) and twelve Bhaavs or houses in the 360-degree elliptic, according to the traditional Jyotishya. Moreover, the 27 Nakshatras or asterisms are connected to the twelve Rashis and houses, with each star getting 13 degrees, 20 minutes in the elliptic. Therefore, every house gets two and a quarter stars, which means that parts of Nakshatra(s) spillover from or into the previous or next Sign or House.

Deviations from Vedic Astrology

The Vedic system is based on the equal house concept, which is the starting point of the deviations in the K. P. System. The K. P. System uses the Placidus System of dividing the Twelve Houses wherein each Cusp of the Twelve Houses—or the beginning of each house—is treated differently and has unique measurements.

The houses' Cusps considered important factors that play a big role in a native's life and life experiences. The measurement of a house could be less than the exact 30 degrees as proposed in Vedic Astrology. Therefore, the Cusp of that particular house will be limited. In fact, in some cases, the Cusp may be entirely missing, and in other cases, two signs might have the same Cusp.

Here is an analogy to explain why further divisions within each star's span to create subdivisions, each with a sub-lord, were needed. Suppose you have a stick that you use as a measuring tool, and you divide and make equal or unequal finite sections on this stick to record the measurements. When you start using this tool, you realize that some hitherto hidden objects or elements are falling between the markings or sections, which can give erroneous measurements. Therefore, you have to make finer subsections of each section to consider the impediments to accurate measurements.

The first sub-division of the span of a star is called Sub. These Subs are again divided into even finer portions referred to as Sub-Sub. The short form is SSL. The next level of sub-divisions is called SS4, and then SS5, and so forth. To measure these Subs and SSLs, Professor Krishnamurthi again used the Dasha system's accepted Vedic form, namely the Vimshottari Dasha System.

According to this ancient, traditional system, each of the nine planets considered in Vedic Astrology has a fixed number of years, during which its Dasha will be played. Each star's span is divided into nine parts, which become the primary Sub-Division. Until now, he followed the Vedic system. Now, he further sub-divided each of these nine parts and obtained one-ninth of a part called Sub-Sub. These sub-divisions are crucial contributing factors for increasing the accuracy of predictions.

Now, a transiting planet is variable because it is continuously moving. The other considerations are Sign-Lord and Star-Lord. The moving planet will occupy one of the nine sub-parts in the star, ruled by one of the nine planets. Therefore, each Sub has a Sub-Lord. When the divisions get finer, there are Sub-Subs, each of which will have a Sub-Sub-Lord, and so forth.

The transiting planet becomes a source of an event. The lord of the star, the sub-lord, the sub-sub-lord, and the lord of the Sign, through which the planet is transiting, will decide the course of events as indicated by the house. It is important to note that the Twelve

Cusps are given the same importance as the planets. Now, every Cusp will have a Cusp-Lord, Star-Lord, and Sub-Lord. Note that the Cusp-Lord will be the Sign-Lord only.

Basic Concepts of K. P. System

An asterism has a fixed length, which is 13 degrees, 20 minutes, or 800 minutes. Each of these asterisms is further divided into nine parts or divisions. Each of these nine divisions (called sub) is again ruled by a planetary lord (called sub-lord). The first ruler is the lord of the constellation himself, followed by the sequence of the lords, according to the Vimshottari Dasha System. Each part's range or span is determined by the years allotted to the planetary lords in the Vimshottari System.

Therefore, 800 minutes is taken as 120 years, which means twenty years is equal to 800 minutes. Therefore, one year is equal to 800/120, which is equal to 20/3. The above formula is used to calculate the spans of the Sub-Lords as follows:

- Ketu rules for seven years in the Vimshottari Dasha System. Converting that using the formula 7 * 20/3), you get 0 degrees, 46 minutes, and 40 seconds.

- Venus or Shukra rules for twenty years. His Sub-Lord Range would be 2 degrees, 13 minutes, and 20 seconds.

- Sun or Surya rules for six years, and therefore, his range would be 0 degrees, 40 minutes.

- Chandra ruling for ten years would have a sub-lord range of 1 degree, 6 minutes, and 40 seconds.

- Mars or Mangala's rule is seven years. The range of his sub-lordship is 0 degrees, 46 minutes, and 40 seconds.

- Rahu (eighteen years) has a sub-lordship range of 2 degrees.

- Jupiter or Guru (sixteen years) has a sub-lordship range of 1 degree, 46 minutes, and 40 seconds.
- Saturn of Shani (nineteen years) has a sub-lordship range of 2 degrees, 6 minutes, and 40 seconds.
- Mercury or Bhuddh (seventeen years) has a sub-lordship range of 1 degree, 53 minutes, and 20 seconds

Therefore, there are twelve signs, 27 Nakshatras, and 249 Subs. Every nine Nakshatra trine sequence consists of 83 Subs in this system. In the K. P. System, the degrees of Chandra and Rahu subs get divided two times in respect of the three trines, which means there are six more Subs, taking the final tally to 249.

Interestingly, in horary Astrology—an ancient form in which the astrologer seeks to find solutions based on the time—the seeker who raised the question asks the questioner to choose a number between 1 and 249, including both. This number given by the questioner is taken as the Lagna and the beginning of the first bhaava.

Ayanamsa is included in the K. P. System calculations and is taken as 50.2388 seconds per year.

Birth charts and horary charts are prepared using the Placidus System, or the semi-arc system. The arc is measured to calculate the Sun's time to rise on a given day at a given latitude. This arc is then divided into three equal divisions. The reason for using this concept is that the rising sun's time places it exactly on the Ascendant.

After that, the Sun transits through the twelfth, eleventh, tenth, etc., at equal intervals until sunset when it reaches the seventh house or the Descendant. In this system, the degrees computed like this are the starting point.

Signs are employed to the strength of the planets and planetary lords. A strong planet will give immediate results, whereas a weak planet takes time to render its effects. Benefic planets in positions of debilitation will act slowly. However, they will not give bad results. Malefic planets in exaltation positions cannot alter bad results to good if their effects are bad. A planet's results are based on its occupation, ownership, and nature.

Also, the planet lord offers results according to the indication given by the Nakshatra Lord in which it is posited. This indicator is more powerful than those given by the house or the planet lord himself. A planet is predominantly under the influence of the Nakshatra lord.

The K. P. System considers that planets are not naturally benefic or malefic. Planets in predominantly improving bhavas, including one, two, three, six, ten, and eleven, give good results, and in the non-improving bhavas, namely four, five, seven, eight, nine, and twelve give bad results. The inherent nature of the planets, however, remains unchanged. Results are experienced only by lords of the dasha, bhukti, and sookshama conjoined together. A Nakshatra lord's results are modified according to the specifications and indications of that planet's sub-lord. Therefore, bad bhava significators are malefic, and good bhava significators are benefic.

In the same way, it is important not to take any house or Sign to be fully malefic or benefic. For example, the sixth house is an improving bhava. *But for what?* is the question asked by the seeker. It is an improving house for getting loans, overdrafts, or service; however, the sixth house is not good for diseases, marriages, etc. The same logic holds good for all the houses. One exception to the rule is that any house twelfth to a house has a negating effect on that house.

Significance of Sub-Lords in K. P. System

So, the range of a constellation is 800 minutes, divided into unequal divisions according to the ruling years allocated to each planet. Professor Krishnamurthi was the first astrologer to have divided this 800-minute range into nine subdivisions, and further divided each of these sub-divisions into sub-sub-divisions. The Nakshatra is analogous to the Dasha periods, the bhukti is analogous to the sub-divisions, and the antardashas are analogous to the Sub-Sub-Lord.

The birth chart can be controlled by the Cusp Sub Lord, who is, in turn, controlled by the Nakshatra lord. This affects the matters determined by the Cusp. The matters dealt with in the houses are modified according to the significations of the cuspal sub lords. Therefore, in the K. P. System, the cuspal sub-lord is the deciding factor.

Therefore, to assess and evaluate questions, the matter in the query should be seen from the perspective of the particular house's cuspal sub-lord, which deals with the matter in question. As an example, the seventh house's Cusp determines the marriage-related matters of the concerned native. If you need to look at children-related matters for a native, you must see the cuspal sub-Lord position of the fifth house, and so forth. Summarily, in the K. P. System of Stellar Astrology, the Cusp of the house and the cusp's sub-lord and his significations are analyzed to make predictions.

Additionally, multiple houses play a role in the life events of a native. The K. P. System has grouped the houses that influence life events together (like a team) and called them House Groups. The primary houses and the supporting houses are combined to get the house grouping for that particular event.

For example, the primary house for good health is the first house, and the supporting house is eleven. Now, the event is promised—in this case, it means the native will enjoy good health—if the sub-lord of the primary house's Cusp signifies both the primary and supporting house. Also, any event's timing is when the planet lords of the ongoing dasha, including the mahadasha, antardasha, and pratyantardasha lords, signify the house group. So, in the example of good health, a native will enjoy good health when he or she passes through the planetary dashas signifying houses one and eleven.

It comes as no surprise that making predictions and reading horoscopes using the K. P. System of Stellar Astrology is more complex than the traditional one, considering that the starting point is the cuspal sub-lord and cannot fit into a small chapter. But the intrigue, mystery, and fascination for this sub-topic of Vedic Astrology cannot be undermined. This bonus chapter is only to trigger an interest so that you learn more about it.

Conclusion

You are likely reeling under the amount of information given in this book about Nakshatras. The data given here is well-researched and tried and tested for centuries. However, do not be disheartened, because the only reason for feeling overwhelmed is that the subject is unfamiliar. Added to that are detailed formulas and mathematical calculations.

Reread the chapters slowly, and the second time around, you will see that it gets easier to follow. Once the wall of difficulty understanding the basics of this fascinating subject falls, it is only an upward trend. You will become so absorbed in it that nothing will stop you from devouring other advanced books and master the topic as fast as you can.

A word of caution is needed at this point. The book has many practical tips for reading the meaning of Nakshatras and their related elements to understand how they work. It is important to know that by itself, this kind of general information is not complete. Every person's Rashi chart and planet transits according to the Dasha systems are individualistic and unique.

Therefore, the information you imbibe from this book must be used in conjunction with the context of individuals' birth charts and their unique Dashas. In fact, it would be a great idea for you to keep your own Rashi Chart and the Dashas developed from your birth chart ready and use it as you learn from this book.

You will be surprised to see how easy you find it to discern the good times and the bad times in your life as you see the movement of the planets through your individual Dasha system under the influence of your birth Nakshatras and other elements related to it. So, go on, read the book, and this time, keep your own Rashi chart with you.

Here's another book by Mari Silva that you might like

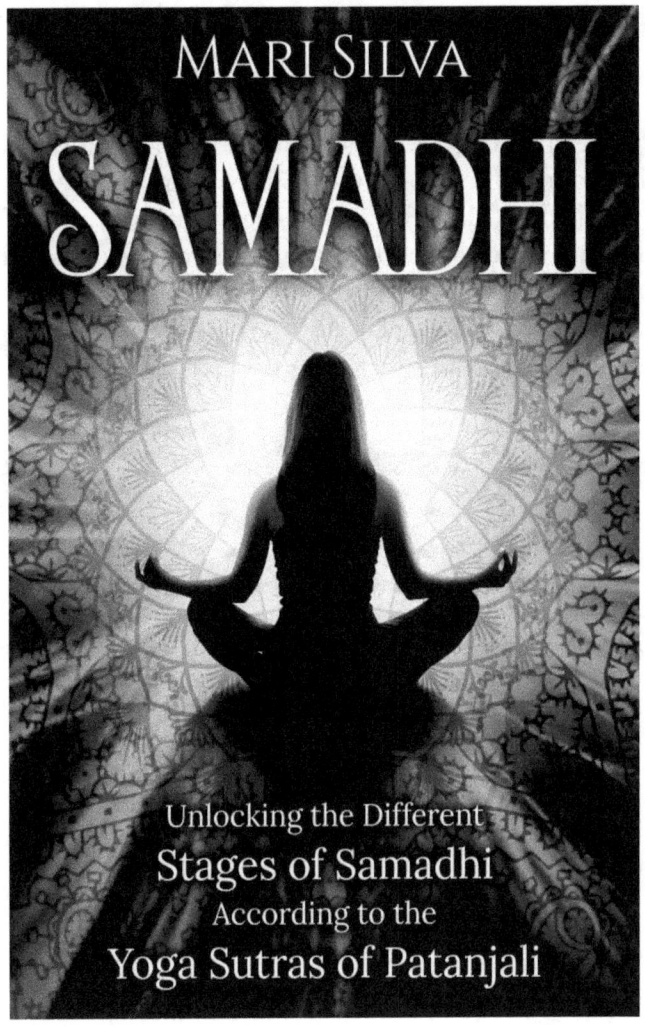

Your Free Gift (only available for a limited time)

Thanks for getting this book! If you want to learn more about various spirituality topics, then join Mari Silva's community and get a free guided meditation MP3 for awakening your third eye. This guided meditation mp3 is designed to open and strengthen ones third eye so you can experience a higher state of consciousness. Simply visit the link below the image to get started.

https://spiritualityspot.com/meditation

Resources

https://www.ganeshaspeaks.com/astrology/nakshatras-constellations/

https://www.astrology-prophets.com/nakshatras.php

https://www.researchgate.net/publication/313163837_28_Nakshatras_-_The_Real_Secrets_of_Vedic_Astrology_An_e-book

https://yogainternational.com/article/view/the-gunas-natures-three-fundamental-forces

https://www.dirah.org/nakshatras.htm

https://www.lunarplanner.com/Astrology/Nakshatras/index.html

https://www.astrologer-astrology.com/constellations_lords_indian_vedic_astrology_jyotish.htm

http://www.jupitersweb.com/star--sub-lord-table.html

https://www.astrojyoti.com/lesson2.htm

http://www.sarvatobhadra.com/janma-nakshatra-birth-star/

https://sites.google.com/site/familykalendars/home/chandrashtamam/janma-anujanma

https://www.astrosoftware.com/27Nakshatra.htm

https://www.selfrealisation.net/UK/VedicAstrology/symbol.htm

https://srath.com/deep-introduction-to-nakshatras/

http://divyanshraizada.blogspot.com/2019/05/nakshatras-major-element-of-vedic.html

https://www.selfrealisation.net/UK/VedicAstrology/symbol.htm

https://www.astrogle.com/astrology/animal-symbols-of-the-nakshatras.html

https://www.templepurohit.com/27-nakshatras-full-nakshatra-names-character-traits/

https://www.astrojyoti.com/phaladeepika9-4.htm

https://www.doyou.com/the-3-types-of-karma-explained/

http://astromuni.com/services/nak.asp

https://binduastrology.com/secrets-of-nakshatra-lordships-and-dasa-systems/

https://www.appliedvedicastrology.com/2018/03/04/nakshatras-secret-transits-power-nine/

https://www.boloji.com/articles/1051/dashas--a-primer

https://www.scribd.com/document/118952001/Ududasha-explanation

https://blog.indianastrologysoftware.com/dashas-and-dasha-periods/

https://www.appliedvedicastrology.com/2020/02/02/secrets-of-dashas-part-1-so-many-secret-techniques-to-get-it-right/

http://www.manyzone.com/article/11110/improve-your-nakshatras-and-stars-in-love-marriage-and-relationships

https://akashvaaniteam.blogspot.com/2018/06/8-things-ashtakoot-guna-milan-can-suggest-you-according-to-janam-kundali.html

https://www.akashvaani.com/blog/ashtakoot-guna-milan-in-a-married-life

https://astrobix.com/astrosight/192-varnadi-ashtakoot-milan-ashtakoot-milan-ashtakoot-guna-milan.html

https://rgyan.com/blogs/career-through-nakshatras-part-1/

https://wealthymatters.com/2013/11/16/nakshatras-and-careers/

https://www.astrolada.com/articles/career-astrology/find-your-career-according-to-the-27-vedic-constellations.html

http://astroworld.co.za/blog/?p=1319%22http://astroworld.co.za/blog/?p=1319

https://www.speakingtree.in/allslides/based-on-your-nakshatras-these-are-the-ideal-career-choices-for-you

https://srath.com/muhurta/

https://www.astrojyoti.com/naksatratithiyogainfo.htm

https://www.astroccult.net/general_muhurats.html

https://www.mahastro.com/how-to-easily-find-an-auspicious-muhurta-ourselves-from-any-vakya-panchangam/

https://karmicrhythms.com/how-to-fix-a-muhurtha-muhurta-panchanga-auspicious-time/

https://www.youtube.com/watch?v=fjeoLYj2021

http://stellarastrology.in/blog/category/astrology/stellar-astrology/

https://www.exoticindiaart.com/book/details/stellar-astrology-and-events-in-life-case-study-approach-to-krishnamurthy-paddhati-NAM237/

https://www.youtube.com/watch?v=HYDnFeKMn8Q

http://www.vaastuinternational.com/KP-Astrology/KP-Astrology.html

www.ingramcontent.com/pod-product-compliance
Lightning Source LLC
Chambersburg PA
CBHW050511240426
43673CB00004B/178